## NatWest Business Handbooks

This series has been written by a team of authors who all have many years' experience and are still actively involved in the day-to-day problems of the small business.

If you are running a small business or are thinking of setting up your own business, you have no time for the general, theoretical and often inessential detail of many business and management books. You need practical, readily accessible, easy-to-follow advice which relates to your own working environment and the problems you encounter. The NatWest Business Handbooks fulfil these needs.

- They concentrate on specific areas which are particularly problematic to the small business.

- They adopt a step-by-step approach to the implementation of sound business skills.

- They offer practical advice on how to tackle problems.

GW00721994

## The author

Maureen Bennett MBA is a small business course co-ordinator at Gloucestershire College of Arts and Technology.

She runs her own business with a partner offering training programmes in accounting for small businesses.

NatWest Business Handbooks

# Managing Growth

## Maureen Bennett MBA

Pitman Publishing
128 Long Acre, London WC2E 9AN
A Division of Longman Group UK Limited

First published in Great Britain in association with the National Westminster Bank,
1989
Reissued in the NatWest Business Handbooks series, 1991

**British Library Cataloguing in Publication Data**
Available on request from the British Library

ISBN 0 273 036254

*The information in this book is intended as a general guide based upon the
legislation at the time of going to press. Neither the Bank, its staff or the author
can accept liability for any loss arising as a result of reliance upon any
information contained herein and readers are strongly advised to obtain
professional advice on an individual basis.*

Typeset, printed and bound in Great Britain

# Contents

# Preface

Whilst personal enterprise is part of a long tradition in the US and many other countries, recent years have seen major government support for enterprise in the UK, initially against a background of high unemployment. The 'enterprise culture' is now therefore a worldwide phenomenon. Business owners everywhere who have survived the start-up stages are daily asking themselves the question: 'How do I make my small business bigger?'. This is a question this book seeks to answer. Growth in all its forms necessitates considerable planning and is likely to involve business and personal risks. The purpose of this book is to provide a practical guide that will help the small business owner who is contemplating growth reduce these risks. Objectives have to be set and decisions made as to the steps that should be taken if the growth is to proceed on a controlled, well-planned basis. The practical nature of the book is reflected not only in the topics chosen but in the manner of their presentation.

The topics are based on matters common to all growth-minded businesses regardless of their sphere of operation. For example manufacturers, retailers and those in service industries have much in common in the key areas of finance, marketing and controls. It is beyond the scope of any book to tackle all problems for all businesses at all stages in the growth process. This book offers a sound basis upon which small business owners can enhance their understanding of growth and the key issues. It brings together essential topics in a clear and readable style.

The author commends the use of checklists and action tasks. Accordingly, these are to be found throughout the book. Addressing these lists and tasks is a rewarding discipline of its own that will increase the reader's business management skills.

The principles behind the book are pertinent to small business owners everywhere and the book does not refer excessively to UK legislation.

Maureen Bennett
Spring 1989

# 1   Making a small business bigger

Where do you stand in the company development cycle? □
Where do you go from here? □ Looking for growth □ The
formula for successful growth □ Conclusion □ Summary

What makes some small firms grow while others have difficulty in achieving even modest expansion? Is it simply luck? Is it being in the right place at the right time? Is it some magical formula known only to a few? Could it be that only certain types, those with entrepreneurial flair, have the vision and foresight to see and grasp opportunities?

There is no magical formula, and whilst a touch of luck may place an individual or company in an opportunistic situation, nothing will actually happen without a great deal of hard work. Some entrepreneurs have more natural flair than others for seeing opportunities, just as some have a natural dedication to work hard. A combination of the two makes for continued business success.

Is your business ready for its next phase on the success ladder, and do you have the vision to proceed? Vision is not entirely dependent on natural flair; it can be developed and improved by constantly feeding it facts and information, gained through internal and external research, which will stimulate ideas and responses. The closer you look at your business and its environment the more likely you are to develop plans for growth which will fit the resources and skills available to you. The purpose of this book is to suggest a number of approaches whereby you can gain information, and to:

- Encourage you to stand back and take a long structured look at your business as it stands.
- Show you how this information can be used to stimulate ideas and discover opportunities for product or market development.
- Examine the strengths of the business so that these might be built on for growth, and to highlight the weaknesses which must be put right.
- Help you discover how to prepare a plan for business expansion.
- Provide information on other important areas related to running a growing business, such as finance, legal aspects, insurance, leadership and personnel.

If you are considering making your business bigger then you will have achieved a measure of success already. Growth may be the route to greater security and a better income. For many the drive to expand is related to gaining satisfaction from achievement, and for some people, many of them millionaires, this need goes on and on. It could be that your business simply needs to expand sufficiently to be able to enjoy greater economies of scale, or to give the edge over the competition. It could mean expanding the workforce from 10 to 20, from 50 to 100, or a whole variety of other things. In this sense growth is a relative term. Consequently a fairly broad approach is adopted in this book, but regardless of how others perceive growth (and how they propose to go about it), you will be seeking to make your own business 'bigger' and this will certainly be a time for reappraisal. Any form of growth is likely to mean that more will be at stake, not least all of the effort in getting you to your present stage.

## Where do you stand in the company development cycle?

All businesses pass through stages of growth, each of which presents a set of problems. Several problems are common to all stages in different degrees. Figure 1.1 outlines the development cycle of a company.

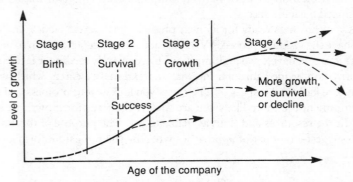

**Fig. 1.1**   Development cycle of a company

At the initial stage business problems include finding start-up finance, premises, first customers and so forth, and in due course a business will begin to emerge. The first few years are precarious and may be concerned almost entirely with survival. Many of the problems are related to finding sufficient finance to service business activity, developing basic administration systems, refining the product or service, and finding staff. The customer base is relatively small and marketing is likely to be very informal. The owner/manager tends to perform both operational and managerial tasks, and is always short of time. During this period growth is slow but steady, and the business becomes increasingly stable.

During the second stage you will have achieved a greater degree of stability, come to terms with basic statutory requirements, established at least basic systems, and expanded both the customer base and the number of employees. It is unlikely that you will have enlarged your range of products or services substantially, or needed to seek new sources of finance, but you may have begun to make greater use of marketing techniques. The demands on your management time will have increased but you may have nothing that resembles a 'management' team in place and this may have prevented a more sophisticated approach to marketing.

## Where do you go from here?

You may seek to widen your customer base and establish a small standardized product line. The aim may be to raise the business to the level of a stable profitable company where the benefits of economies of scale can be introduced into the production processes. You will expand the number of employees, introducing technical expertise as required. The main problem at this stage is the transition of the owner/manager from operational management to business management. Many entrepreneurs find this a difficult and painful process, but success is very dependent on their making the change. The owner/manager must be able to stand back and to delegate, thus allowing time for managing and decision-making. The need to develop a management team is increasingly urgent as the number of staff grows and the customer base gets bigger.

At some point you will need to make a decision. Should you take the route to further expansion or remain stable and profitable by not increasing in size any further? The decision is very much related to the type of business you are in, and to your personal aims and objectives. A business which operates in a dynamic market place, for example high technology, has greater opportunities for more rapid and greater growth than one in a static or stable market, such as retail shoes or butchery. However, growth can be in degrees, and most businesses are capable of some growth.

## Looking for growth

Your business may have already moved into the success stage and you may be running a company with an established credibility and proven technical capability. The need to delegate may have increased and a small management team may have formed or at least be beginning to take shape. In one sense this early growth position is not unlike the pre-birth of your company when you planned and researched the threats and the opportunities before committing yourself to the actual business launch.

The third stage of business development involves growing from a small stable and successful business into a larger organization which has to tackle a number of new problems. Suddenly control and information systems are inadequate to cope with growing needs, and there may be unforeseen liquidity problems related to capital and funding requirements. Greater investment means greater risk and there is the need to evaluate the risk against market opportunities. There is an urgent need for planning in all areas of the business. These are summarized below.

(a)   A more formal management team will need to be developed. It is necessary to delegate responsibilities related to the technical and operational aspects. Leadership skills are increasingly important.

(b)   Staff levels are likely to grow and the whole system will become more formalized. Employees will have expectations of salaries, conditions, contracts, rights and training.

(c)   Production facilities and activities may be inadequate and under-staffed. It will be necessary to plan capacity levels, schedules, costings, skills, etc., so that output is capable of meeting demand at the right price and at the right time.

(d)   Finance becomes a main concern as the business starts to grow. There is often a need for further capital investment and loans to cover expansion of fixed assets and increased working capital needs.

(e)   The market and the business environment will need researching in order to seek new product or market development.

(f)   Competitor analysis is an important aspect of planning. You will need to assess their likely response to your own increased activity in the market place, and to make strategic plans to keep them at bay.

The growth process is different for every business. There will be specific factors which are critical to your own organization's success. For instance, finding staff with the right skills and the right personal qualities may be a key factor for your business. There may be a need for greater capacity if machines are old and space is limited. These key areas where things must go right are different for every business, so it is important to discover what these are at the beginning.

## The formula for successful growth

The authors of a booklet called *Make Ready for Success* researched 350 firms in the print trade, which is characterized by a large number of small firms. From their research they arrived at a formula for success which could well be adopted as a blueprint for growth for any small firm.

1. Define your business objectives and operate to meet them.
2. Identify market opportunities and co-ordinate commercial effort to achieve planned results.
3. Obtain a clear understanding of money and its use as a company resource.
4. Install good decision-making procedures and supporting information systems.
5. Organize your management to operate as a team, and to enable managers to be developed and trained to meet the changing needs of the business.

Source: *Make Ready for Success*, published by the National Economic Development Office.

## Conclusion

This book endeavours to help you find answers to the issues raised in this chapter. At the end of several chapters there are suggested action tasks which outline ways in which you might tackle the research needed for the planning processes. Checklists are also added throughout the book. These are designed to stimulate thought and discussion in readiness for decision-making or planning.

## Summary

Small business are more likely to get bigger and continue to succeed if there is a positive commitment to growth. This means that the owner-manager and his or her team will allocate time to getting involved in researching opportunities and developing plans which will allow the business to build on its strengths.

Growth is a relative term. Your firm sees expansion from its own position on the company development cycle, therefore the growth process is different for every firm. Your choice between stability and further growth will be influenced by (a) personal objectives, (b) business objectives, and (c) the type of business you are in.

There are critical success factors which are specific to your own business, and these need to be identified early on. These might, for example, include a need for certain types of skills.

The formula for success includes setting objectives, planning and co-ordinating marketing activities, understanding money, setting up systems, and organizing a management team.

# 2  Growth is about ...

Size □ Turnover and profitability □ Customer base □ Exporting □ Planning the product or service □ Developing or buying another business □ Buying a business □ Finding the money □ Coping with change □ Planning ahead □ Summary □ Checklist

Most business owners have some ideas on the subject of expansion. However, many rush headlong into their next phase of activity with nothing more than an idea, and with very little in the way of structured planning. Then they continue to run the business on a crisis basis, shunting along from problem to problem, usually in the areas of cash, customers, suppliers and staff.

The well-established small business which is showing a steady increase in profits and has a good management base is ready for growth. As the owner or manager you will have to consider both personal and economic objectives in deciding on the style and direction your firm will take in the next five years or so. In order to set up your expansion project you will need to undertake research into the firm, its resources, the market place and the environment. This will take considerable time and organization, and in itself is a good test of the availability of management skills. It is also a good learning exercise for those involved.

To grow or not to grow? Some business owners will have reached a size where they feel that further expansion will mean loss of control and the personal touch, but it is important to realize that no business can stand still in today's rapidly changing economy. There are always predators in the form of similar businesses entering the market place, therefore some growth is necessary if only to deal with the competition.

So what exactly do we mean by growth?

## Size

For many owner/managers growth means getting larger in size by expanding the existing business. This could entail taking over the premises next door, or moving to a bigger factory and employing more people. For others it means starting up a branch or similar business in the next town or district, with the owner working very hard managing them both. Either approach offers the advantage of being able to use existing knowledge of both product and market.

## Turnover and profitability

You may be in a position where your firm is making profits but is not producing to full capacity, in which case growth probably means setting higher sales targets and increasing turnover. The extra margin can be achieved without any great increase in fixed overheads.

It is an interesting fact that most business owners can quote turnover figures and turnover targets, but rarely quote profit figures. In fact many seem to be obsessed with size of turnover to a point of vanity. High turnover does not necessarily equate to high profitability. For example, a service-based firm with a turnover of £80,000 may have a net profit margin of 50%, i.e. £40,000 profit, whilst a product-based firm is more likely to have a net margin of 20% and would need a turnover of £200,000 to make the same profit.

If your business sells only one product then the sums are relatively simple – you can quickly work out costs and profit. However, most firms sell a range of products or services, and the bigger the range the more difficult it becomes to identify the best product mix to produce and sell. A number of factors come into consideration such as:

- Contribution (to profits or costs) of each type of product.
- Customer demand, seasonal patterns, special needs.
- Knowing the fixed costs of the business.
- Pricing the products correctly.
- Storage space requirements.

Costing, pricing and product mix are very important aspects of marketing and controlling the business. They are discussed in greater detail in later chapters.

---

A Gloucestershire business owner told me that at the end of her first year of trading she achieved a turnover of £150,000. I was suitably impressed, then she added, 'I have just received my first year's accounts and I made a £25,000 loss. I am now three months into my second year, what can I do about it?'

In other words, £150,000 had flowed into the business and £175,000 had flowed out! How could anyone sell their goods at less than they paid for them and not be aware of it? Quite easily – this often happens in creative situations where the producer is 'in love' with the product and cannot bring himself to 'sacrifice quality' by proper buying and costing of materials and time.

In this particular case the business had several positive aspects. Demand for the product was high, prices were the highest in the county, the style was fairly unique, and the service was excellent. Fortunately the problems were simple to identify and rectify. These included overstaffing (employing friends), lack of costing, and an inexperienced buyer who was a salesman's dream. The firm is now five years old, continually profitable, and growing steadily.

## Customer base

2

Having a larger customer base is usually seen as an aim for a growing company. For example, a small packaging firm will grow within a certain geographical radius and is unable or unwilling to service requests outside that area because of the volume of business it can cope with, and the extra costs involved with distance. Eventually competition will force the business to consider growth by expanding geographically, and by expanding the product range within the same market place.

A decision to expand may be based on the current demand level which cannot be met from existing resources. This is an ideal situation, and one which should be exploited before the competition moves in to fill the gap. On the other hand it may be felt that with greater sales effort more turnover can be achieved with the same customers. For either approach the prerequisite is an evaluation of future sales and the financial implications related to the expansion. The starting point is an in-depth analysis of existing customers. In the following chapter we will consider ways of finding the necessary information which will define the customer in terms of demand, needs, location, spending power, etc.

The opposite and more hazardous route to growth is to enter into 'the Marks & Spencer syndrome', i.e. finding a single large customer whose needs absorb most of the skills and resources of the company to such an extent that the organization becomes solely dependent on the key customer, who is then placed in a very powerful position. In this situation, the loss of one large order is sometimes sufficient to put the small firm out of business.

## Exporting

The single European Market may offer the challenge of a bigger customer base, and could be the stimulus for preparations for growth. Existing trade barriers will be removed by the end of 1992, thus providing greater opportunity to sell to new customers and to develop new products and services for new markets.

If you are aiming to export for the first time to the European Community, or further afield, you will need to set up a sound organization basis. The management structure should be such that it is capable of exploiting new opportunities as they arise. Training in languages and other skills may be necessary, and a review of cash resources and credit availability is vital.

The most critical decision is *how* we enter foreign markets. This is influenced by the degree of control the company is allowed over the product once it arrives in the foreign market, and the ability to take all the marketing decisions which subsequently have to be taken.

There are two variables to consider, production in the home market and exporting either directly or indirectly, or setting up a production unit within the foreign market. These are illustrated in Fig. 2.1.

Western Europe is an affluent and highly developed market. With a population five times that of the UK, and six times the buying power, it is geographically close and virtually tariff free. Other European competitors are exploiting these advantages by treating neighbouring countries as extensions of their home markets.

The decision to export is a decision to expand the scope and nature of your business, which means that the amount of research and preparation undertaken, and the commitment of cash and resources, are vital. If the business is very small, and resources such as management, production and finance are already stretched then the time may not be right for you just yet.

There are a number of organizations ready to give help and advice on all aspects of exporting. These include the British Overseas Trade Board (BOTB), Chambers of Commerce, export clubs, banks, trade associations, Technical Help for Exporters (THE), and many others. HMSO publish a range of slim volumes on exporting to different countries, which describe in brief how to do it, and provide very useful lists of names and addresses.

An excellent in-depth treatment of exporting for small businesses is to be found in James W. Dudley's *Exporting*, also published in this series.

## Planning the product or service

You may have decided that the product, *whether a tangible item or a service*, is the key to expansion – you have something to sell. In this case it becomes necessary to emphasize that your whole approach to the style, qualities, presentation and uses of your product must be one of total

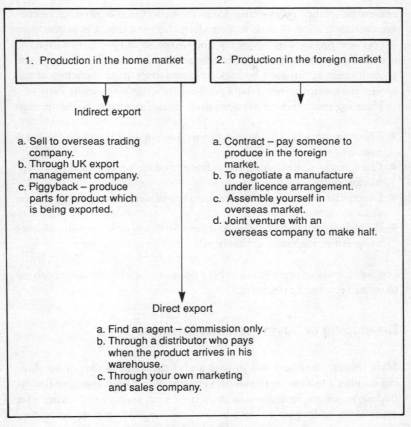

**Fig. 2.1** Routes to exporting

flexibility. In other words, the attributes of your product must be constantly reviewed in the light of your customers' needs and wants. You will therefore have to develop acute 'listening' skills in order to:

(a) assess customer expectations, which are constantly changing, and
(b) gain the edge over your competitors.

The product is a very important aspect of the whole marketing package. Each product has a life cycle of growth, maturity and decline; some life cycles are very short, for example pop records, other products will continue for several years. Therefore making wise product decisions depends on discovering and understanding the benefits your existing customers perceive in your products, searching for opportunities, and a reasonable ability for picking front runners. Once a product reaches satisfaction level it is time to introduce the next one. Customers now expect new products more quickly, and will reject old products with equal speed. Tomorrow's markets are the realm of business survivors, and growth must be fostered by backing tomorrow's products while at the same time ensuring that today's products continue to generate cash.

Planning your products could mean choosing from a number of options:

- The introduction of a new product to the range for the same customer base.
- Changing or embellishing the current product, perhaps adding an up-market range.
- Diversifying skills and resources into a totally different product for the same or different markets.
- Reducing the product range and concentrating on increasing market share either regionally or nationally.

Chapter 5 looks in more detail at how product planning should be related to overall marketing objectives.

## Developing or buying another business

Many owner/managers seek growth and challenge by buying or developing another business alongside the existing one. Often the new firm is trading in a complementary or associated way, such as the owner of a delicatessen setting up an outside catering company, or a garden centre offering garden design services and landscape gardening. This provides the opportunity to use some of the same resources and skills.

Another approach, known as vertical integration, involves setting up a business doing the things which either your customers or suppliers do for example a menswear retailer setting up a manufacturing unit to produce 'own label' suits, or a bakery opening a shop for its products. In this case the aim is to gain greater profit opportunities from both activities, as well as ensuring supply or a distribution outlet.

Buying an existing business may be the quickest route for achieving growth in that the firm is already set up with equipment, employees, customers and track record. This may offer the opportunity for the same type of business in another location, or a complementary business in the same location, or even a chance for vertical integration. However, there are a number of important factors involved in buying an existing business and professional advice should be sought from a surveyor, solicitor, accountant and bank manager. A very careful appraisal should be undertaken and a detailed plan of action needs to be drawn up before any contracts are signed. Areas for consideration will include:

(a) Land and property, their condition, location, market value, title, access, licences, leases, financial encumbrances against the property.

(b) Stock – you must work out an agreed formula for valuation.

(c) Creditors and loans must be investigated – what kind of reputation does the business have with suppliers and bankers?

(d) Goodwill may be two to four times the net profit figure – find the norm for the type of business. Is the business particularly dependent on the skill, reputation or personal contacts of the present manager? If so can they be acquired by you?

(e) 'Key money' has no value and is simply a premium for obtaining the lease – can it be negotiated down?

(f) Staff – their attitudes to a new boss and possible change. Labour availability.

(g) Accounts for previous years, books and bank statements should be audited by your accountant.

(h) The asking price, which is usually net assets plus goodwill and/or key money.

## Buying a business

1. Does the business match your training, experience and temperament?
2. Can you afford to undertake the capital requirement?
3. What are the growth possibilities for the business?
4. What are you actually buying – physical assets, goodwill, momentum?
5. Could the assets be acquired more cheaply by starting a new business than by buying this one?
6. Is the business a profitable investment at the asking price?

## Finding the money

'If only I could raise the cash!' How often have you watched an opportunity pass by because of lack of funds? Growing businesses usually need considerable financial investment. Banks are in the business of lending money, that is how they make their profits, but your bank manager will not take unnecessary risks with investors' funds. If your business is well established and efficiently run then you will have a good track record with the bank. Therefore a well presented and sound project, combined with tenacity on your part, will usually result in the necessary loan or overdraft being granted.

Unfortunately, a great many businesses are run rather less efficiently, or have been started with insufficient cash levels, which leads to a record of cash flow problems, even though the order book is full. In this situation an expansion opportunity is less likely to inspire the bank's confidence. Unfortunately the records show that many growing and potentially profitable businesses go under because they run out of cash – this is known as 'overtrading' and is explained in Chapter 8. Then there is the 'cosmetic' business plan, which takes the form of a beautifully prepared document produced with the specific aim of getting funds, and afterwards filed away forever. Owners themselves are often so impressed with the rosy picture presented that when things go wrong they are apt to blame the bank manager for giving them the money!

Of course the bank is not the only source of funds, and we will look at finance in greater detail in Chapter 9. The point of this section is to emphasize that as owner/manager wishing to expand the business it is useful to keep in mind that you are the bank's customer and that the bank manager will frequently prove to be an important listening post for you. He or she will help you stay abreast of economic conditions in the community, will get credit information for you on prospective customers, and will follow the progress of your business with honest interest and offer advice when it seems likely to be useful.

## Coping with change

Growth can come about in a number of ways, e.g. internal change, additional staff, bigger premises, acquisition of another company, merger, forming a partnership. Everyone in the company is affected by the changes. There will be new systems to learn, new skills to acquire, new staff to relate to. Some people will be relinquishing responsibilities, and managers will have to delegate some of their tasks. A more formal structure should emerge, and as a result, some of the flexibility may disappear.

You and your management team must be able to set up new systems and manage staff, as well as set targets, assess and reassess funding, control profit margins, undertake market and product development, look after the premises, keep an eye on the competition, and so on. Coping with these changes means that you will have to ensure that staff are sufficiently trained to give the support needed. Your whole programme will require strong leadership and a good management team.

Often those who occupy managerial or supervisory roles in small firms concentrate their energies on specific skills-related functions, like production, while the real job of managing is undertaken by one person, usually the owner/manager. This is a legacy of the very small firm where the owner tends to make all his own decisions and often carries all the information in his head. Businesses employing up to ten people can just about survive with one level of management, but the personnel aspects are often fraught with stress and difficulties, and the firm's performance level suffers as a result. Any greater expansion requires the formation of a management team and an organizational structure. Team building and leadership are discussed in Chapter 13.

## Planning ahead

Small businesses are usually based on the owner's area of technical skills and expertise. Engineers form engineering companies, computer experts sell computer expertise, and so on. As a result most small firms have become established through personal contacts and local knowledge. Growth to date has probably come about by early marketing activity and word of mouth. Your business may have reached a plateau where you find yourself complaining about one or more of the following:

- Working seven days a week and still no richer.
- Not knowing whether there will be any future orders.
- Too many orders now but ...
- Needing to employ staff but unsure of the future.
- Short of funds for staff and capital items.
- Bored and looking for a challenge.

Most of these situations are caused by the owner/manager's inability or reluctance to stand back and look objectively at where the business is going, and to make the transition from production expert to management co-ordinator.

Business growth brings with it the need for a new approach to running a business. If your aim is to maximize profits you must set aside one or two days per week for management and marketing related activities. Setting goals, researching ways of meeting the needs of the customers, encouraging teamwork and organizing activity are all part of the package.

In order to set achievable objectives and design future strategies it is important to carry out a realistic appraisal of your firm's current position. This will involve assessing strengths and weaknesses in terms of skills and resources, researching the market place, analysing the needs of existing and potential customers, and identifying the competition. Once this has been done certain quantifiable objectives can be set and a marketing plan drawn up.

The aim of the following chapters of this book is to provide a practical guide to planning growth. It is suggested that you work through the activity lists. Use the checklists as a help in researching the business.

## Summary

Growth means increasing profits.

Businesses take different routes towards achieving this goal. The choice is related to personal aspirations and abilities, demand, finance, location, product specifications, and searching for opportunities.

Looking for further business development and improving your profits will mean planning markets, product mix, sales and distribution, pricing, management and finance.

Many small businesses will see exporting as a route to growth. The 1992 single market may stimulate further growth preparation.

The rest of this book is aimed at helping you to review your business as it stands, and to develop a strategic plan for the future.

## Checklist

---

1. Are you in business to make money?
2. Is your main reason for being in business your desire and liking for independence?
3. Are you seeking to create a 'family business' to pass on to the family?
4. Are you seeking to build up a saleable business with a view to 'cashing in' at an opportune moment (e.g. retirement)?
5. Are you driven by the desire to give a service?
6. What is your attitude to risk? Are you seeking the excitement associated with the 'first in the field' approach?
7. Have you been content to adopt a 'follow my leader' approach?
8. Do you wish to run a 'stable small business'?
9. Do you wish to expand and develop the business?
10. Are any growth ambitions in any way constrained by your personal objectives? (For example, would you be prepared to trade off some independence and control in favour of growth?)
11. Can your business objectives be expressed in terms of size of turnover, number of outlets, size of workforce, return on capital or in any other measurable way?
12. Do you wish to expand the range of products or services?

---

# 3   Where are we now?

What business are you in? □ Who are your customers? □ What influences customer choice? □ What is the product or service? □ The product portfolio □ How strong is the product? □ Who are your competitors? □ Summary □ Checklist

Planning ahead is fundamental to business growth and long-term survival. In this chapter we will consider ways of appraising the current position of the firm, and its potential for development. At this stage we are seeking to establish *where we are now* and *where we want to be*, and what steps we must take in terms of skills, resources and time planning to get there.

Management time is a scarce resource, and as a small business owner, you will be heavily involved in the day-to-day operation of the business. However, it is important that you recognize the present need to commit time to steering the business towards achieving your objectives. Up-to-date information is needed for the decision-making process, therefore some measure of research, updating and analysis will be necessary before a comprehensive plan can be formulated. At this point it must be stressed that an objective approach is needed in seeking accurate data, both inside and outside the business.

Key factors in the assessment process are:

- The reasons for the exercise, i.e. the objectives.
- The amount of management time available.
- Ability to explore external and internal information sources.
- Objectivity in making assessments.
- Communication skills.

## What business are you in?

This may seem relatively simple to answer, but beware, the question is about policy as well as product, and considerable time should be given to assessing the market place your business operates in, and who exactly your competitors are.

This is best illustrated by an example. A company manufacturing pen nibs in the 1940s may have stated, 'We are in the stainless steel pen nib business, and our customers are stationers, offices and educational institutions; we compete with other steel pen nib producers.' This short-sighted statement does not describe the real market place from the end user's point of view, i.e. the needs of the student, author, secretary, etc., nor does it correctly pinpoint the competition.

However, by identifying the 'communications business' and its immediate needs of speed, portability, compactness, appearance, etc., the creator of the ball-point pen effectively wiped out the early pen nib market. The producer of this new-fangled pen had not been identified as a competitor to pen nib manufacturers, partly because the product had been developed in a different material, i.e. plastic. Nevertheless here was a real competitor who had approached the communications market place in an innovative and creative style. Since then ball-point and fountain pens have changed in style and presentation, and are heavily promoted in the 'gift trade'.

Another interesting example of good lateral thinking is the manager of the local garden centre who states categorically that he is in the home furnishing business. Theodore Levitt, the great educator, summed it up – 'When a customer buys a quarter inch drill he wants a quarter inch hole.'

Technological advancement makes the modern business world even more hazardous for the small business because the product or service can be developed or overtaken by innovation from many directions. It becomes increasingly important to examine the business and range of markets you are in, in order to help determine targets for sustainable, internally generated growth from product and/or market diversification.

The business owner who is thinking about expansion has already established that there is a reasonable market for the product or service. When the business is small, local market information and spotting market gaps comes largely from personal contacts. This usually causes problems when moving into bigger markets. Before committing more effort and resources to business growth it would be wise to take stock of the current situation in terms of your existing customers, the competition, the company's cash management, and the skills and resources available.

---

Before progressing to more detailed research write down your responses to the following questions:

1. Describe your product(s) or services in detail.
2. Can you clearly define the market segment, or segments, your business serves?
3. Have you spotted a gap in the market?
4. Does your business have specific skills which you wish to exploit?
5. Are you looking for new customers for existing products?
6. Are you planning to add to your product range?

---

## Who are your customers?

Business survival is about satisfied customers, so clearly you need to examine the profile of your existing customers, and to estimate your share of the market. This raises a number of questions. Are we meeting customer needs? Is demand changing? What are the trends?

Small firms, by definition, have smaller market shares than their larger competitors. Often the parameters are set by territory and the customer base is limited. The fundamental strategy for the small firm which is planning growth is to concentrate all of its efforts on one area of the market at a time, rather than spread limited resources too thinly over the whole market. Once established, the next stage of growth, in another defined segment, can be planned.

### Market segments

Every market is made up of segments of buyers each with different needs, buying styles and responses to different types of offers. Your aim must be to identify target groups who have distinctive patterns of needs, and to develop products or services to meet their needs. This will provide the cornerstone for your total planning. You must start by defining your existing customer profile, i.e. who are your customers? Why do they buy from you? Can you sell them more? Are there more of them?

The research of market segments raises a number of positive points about how to maintain or improve the market share for existing products, and how to make inroads into the market of competitive brands. It also helps identify other needs through which the product base can be expanded, and may point to other markets for both existing and new products. By defining the customer much more exactly there is a much better chance of making the advertising and promotion count.

No small firm is ready for growth until, by way of internal and external research, it has defined its existing and target customers in such a way that each segment is separately specified and the differing needs of each group understood. There is no unique way to segment a market. One method used to segment the consumer market, is to divide the population into target groups.

### Factors for segmenting consumer groups

- *Socio-economic group*. The population is divided into groups based on educational/professional/social backgrounds:

A/B   Professional and managerial
C1    Clerical and supervisory
C2    Skilled manual workers
D     Unskilled manual workers
E     Unemployed/OAPs

Newspapers use this method. The *Guardian* aims at ABs, the *Sun* and *Mirror* at C1s and C2s, the *Star* at C2s, Ds and Es.

- *Income group*. This is slightly different to socio-economic group, i.e. a C2 household often has a higher disposable income than a C1 or B household.

- *Age/sex/marital status/family size*. For example, the youth market subdivides into infant market, teenage market, college market, etc.

- *Culture/ethnic group*.

- *Geographical areas*. For example, in the UK the South East is the most populated (30%) and the most affluent. Sub-segments are regions, climate, city and city densities.

- *Personality variables*. Attempts have been made to segment by behaviour: (a) aggressive; (b) passive; (c) compulsive; (d) leaders.

- *Value perceptions or social aspirations*. For example, the motives for buying a car could be various: for economy, or for utility, or for reliability, or perhaps for image (prestige), or for special performance, or the desire to identify with a particular social or income group.

- *Usage rate*. For example, light/regular/heavy/occasional users.

---

Researching industrial markets, i.e. for firms who provide a product or service to other firms, is rather more specific. The customer base is usually quite small, although there may be many potential users. The customer will often have specialist knowledge of the product and is quite clear about his own needs. On the whole the industrial customer is prepared to co-operate in discussing product specifications, price and service arrangements, and sometimes will discuss the competition.

## Internal data

You should be particularly interested in the characteristics of your existing customers and the size of your share of the potential market. For this purpose past customers should also be analysed in order to find out why you lost them, and what must be done to win them back. There is a need for key data, and the most available source of data is company records.

It should be possible to find historical figures for total *sales, costs and profits*, and the sales ledger will provide *customer details*. Our objective is to examine customer behaviour by discovering *what* is bought and *why*. We also wish to identify any groups of products which are growing, static or declining, where opportunities are, and where problems lie. Categories might include:

- Number of customers
- Volume and value of purchases
- Pattern of purchases (seasons, cycles, etc.), frequency of purchase
- Physical characteristics of products
- Place of purchase
- Price paid
- Credit risk
- Key customers
- Trends during preceding years.

If your company has a management system which is based on analysing products by *contribution* it will be possible to assess which products and customers are most profitable, and to gain an indication of where to concentrate effort.

## External data

Once internal data has been sifted and used there are a number of publicly available statistics which will aid the research and provide different views of the market place and its environment. Most can be found in public libraries and will include the following:

- *The Family Expenditure Survey* (HMSO). Gives estimates of national and regional expenditure on particular products and services, household composition, accommodation, ownership, income from all sources, etc. Very detailed.
- *Employment Gazette* (HMSO). Provides data on the labour market: employment, unemployment, vacancies, disputes, earnings and retail prices. Includes news and features on aspects of employment and government announcements.
- *General Household Survey* (HMSO). Very detailed data on housing, employment, education, health, family structure and leisure patterns.
- *Regional Trends* (HMSO). Covers statistics for geographical regions on: housing, employment, distribution, transport, personal incomes

and household expenditure. Many county councils and larger cities have started producing their own local statistical compilations.

- *Social Trends* (HMSO). Covers most aspects of social life and social change in UK. Presented in bright format. Carries articles by statisticians interpreting the social changes which the statistics are signalling.
- *Census of Population* (HMSO). Covers the most recent census for the whole population. Broken down into national, regional, county, district, constituency, ward and civil parish level. Includes topic reports for the country.
- *Overseas Trade Statistics of the United Kingdom*. Gives detailed figures for imports and exports arranged by total figures for each month and the year to date; by area of country; by commodity.
- *Marketing Intelligence* (MINTEL). Monthly marketing intelligence on a whole range of consumer goods. General reports on specific areas, e.g. mineral waters. In-depth reports on chosen topics can be purchased.
- *Reference manuals, directories, e.g. Kompass.* Provide company listings, capital and consumer goods producers, services.

There are other government sources such as the *Annual Abstract of Statistics*, *British Business*, *Business Monitor* series, *Economic Trends*, and *Financial Statistics*, which can provide background to any research project.

Useful, often free, information can also be obtained from the regional Small Firms Services, the Rural Development Commission, local enterprise agencies, chambers of commerce and banks. The British Overseas Trade Board (BOTB) provides information and services for exporters. Read what you can in trade newspapers and business magazines about your own and similar competitive products.

There are also research organizations which produce regular information on specific market areas. The Economic Intelligence Unit (EIU), A. C. Nielsen, Audits of Great Britain (AGB) and Textile Market Studies all produce reports and surveys for the retail trade, consumer products, and the textile and clothing industries.

It may be difficult to find population figures for your precise product, but there is often a relationship between a product and a set of figures. For example, a computer-aided kitchen design service could make use of the following obtainable information:

- Size of local population, its breakdown into age, sex, occupation.
- Number of houses, new houses, estates.
- Local expenditure on DIY.
- Number of architects, builders, kitchen suppliers.

## Example

La Parisienne is a small cosmetics firm. They have produced a new cosmetic for women with dry skin, and are considering a number of factors before making the decision on whether to launch the product.

1. There are 28,321,400 women in the United Kingdom.
2. Deduct those under nineteen who are less likely to be troubled by dry skin. Experienced cosmetic marketers find the fifty plus a tough market to sell to. Brand loyalties among older women are hard to change. This leaves *12,486,000*.
3. The product should be packaged and promoted as a high fashion item, so is unlikely to be stocked by shops in rural areas. Therefore distribution problems will reduce the number to *10,971,000*.
4. Price will also serve to reduce the market. The cream is going to be expensive to make and sell, and only women with a fairly high income will be able to afford it. A family income of £18,000 a year or more would probably be necessary. This reduces the figure to *2,708,000*.
5. There is no census for women with dry skin. A sample survey, perhaps to beauticians or house-to-house will have to be undertaken. We learn that 10% of the women in the 19–50 age group suffer from dry skin to the extent that they are willing to buy a high priced product. The figure is now *270,800*.
6. Other dry skin creams are advertised, which have strong brand names, and even though our new product is vastly superior it would be optimistic to assume that even a quarter would buy the new product. That leaves a maximum of *67,700*.
7. There is always the problem of persuading the stockists to carry a line which will only make a few sales, and competing with several other well-known brands. The potential may not be great enough to support promotion and distribution costs which may be prohibitive.

## Ask the people

The employees of your company can provide very useful information about the market. Sales staff, delivery drivers and stores people are often in direct contact with customers, and should be encouraged to observe and glean information, not only about needs, but about the strengths and weaknesses of others who supply the same customers.

The very best class of market information is that which is gained directly from the customers since it tells us the process by which their needs have been satisfied and what other requirements they have. The owner/manager needs to devise a means of making direct contact with a sufficient number of clients to provide a clear picture about product expectations, the firm's reputation, customers' suggestions, and how the firm and the product compare with the competition.

This kind of market research is often carried out by interview, based on a short well-designed questionnaire; however, the process can consume considerable time and money. The questionnaire can be sent out by mailshot but the quality of response is often unreliable. Telephone interviewing is becoming increasingly popular because it is quick and relatively cheap, and a large number of interviews can be carried out in a day. Other approaches include joining business clubs and chambers of commerce, or attending shows, exhibitions and places where your customers are likely to congregate.

Information, gathered formally or informally, must establish the needs and satisfaction levels of the customers, and indicate opportunities for increasing and developing competitive advantage. Remember that the ultimate aim is business expansion. Having segmented the market, the firm must translate this information into plans for the type and style of product or service to be provided, how it will be promoted, and what pricing policy to adopt.

Some small firms believe that the customer sees the market as a set of products all equally suitable for his purpose. This leads to the belief that price alone is important to the customer. Market segmentation helps move away from this erroneous assumption, and enables the owner/ manager to use price as a marketing tool. This theme is explored further in Chapter 7, *Pricing for Profits*.

## What influences customer choice?

The small firm which takes a marketing approach finds opportunities by seeking groups or segments whose needs it wishes to serve, thus fulfilling the basic objectives which are to provide satisfaction for customers, and in the process generate sufficient revenue and profits. Market research is aimed at identifying segments and the factors which influence choice, i.e. style, quality, design, convenience, service and price: variables which can be adjusted to suit the customer's needs.

The customer is influenced in his choice by a combination of factors which are often different to those specified by the producer. For example, a company selling additive-free food products which are delivered to the consumer might expect the customer to rate 'healthy eating' as the key selling issue, but might find that 'convenience' was just as important, especially to those customers in rural areas. You must visualize your product or service in terms of a range of benefits to the customer – this is what he or she is buying – a solution to a problem. Thus a product is a combination of factors, a 'bundle of satisfaction' or benefits, and must be regarded as flexible, and subject to change and development.

It must be added that a purchaser does not only make his choice based on the function of the product and its ability to perform the task; he is also swayed by his perceptions of non-functional factors such as brand image, price associations, personal image, status, etc.

Marketing a service is not very different from marketing a product. The main difference is that benefits cannot be stored. The person providing the service is usually the key factor. The customer is buying reliability and professional competence, and is often prepared to pay a higher price for better individual attention to his needs. Therefore it is vital to market the personal qualities of key staff and employees in order to establish the right image.

## What is the product or service?

Most small firms are started because someone has something to sell, i.e. a product or service. It is now appropriate to undertake an appraisal of these products as part of the marketing exercise. Which of your products are expanding, and which are declining? Every product has its own life cycle of growth, maturity, saturation and decline, and this produces implications for new product strategies, since sooner or later every product is either pre-empted by another, or else degenerates into profitless competition. It would be naive to assume that every product displayed a pattern similar to the 'typical' life cycle; some enjoy longer periods, shorter periods, or even recycles.

### The product life cycle

New products consume cash and create risk. At the introductory stage much time and money is spent on creating awareness and finding the best means of reaching the customer. The complete lack of customer loyalty means that growth potential is often difficult to predict.

As the product/service moves into the growth stage customer loyalty grows, and the market becomes more stable. Suppliers will allow discounts on bulk material purchases and there is rapid expansion in production, which sometimes means prices can be dropped. Competitors will be attracted by your obvious growth and apparent high margins, but there is still new business available. Levels of demand become clearer and it is now possible to generate sales forecasts with greater accuracy. Technology becomes vital in areas of production. Costs per unit decrease significantly as machinery and staff perform to greater capacity, and the organization becomes more efficient with experience.

Once the life cycle curve (see Fig. 3.1) starts to level off, some of the marginal competitors have dropped out. The market share remains stable and there are well developed buying patterns with plenty of customer loyalty. Product requirements in terms of process and materials are well known and relatively undemanding. New competitors now have to 'win' business away from established companies. Often new technology is introduced in a thrust to renew the industry. Potential demand is now well defined.

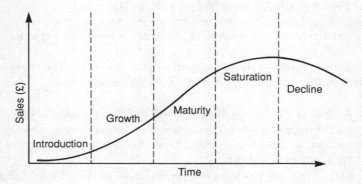

**Fig. 3.1** The product life cycle

Eventually customers' needs change and the market starts to decline. Growth potential is limited and the less profitable lines are dropped.

Your overall objective is to balance sales growth, cash flow and risk, in order to grow profitably over a period of time. Looking at individual products in terms of place in the life cycle helps focus your attention on the need to take action regularly in order to maintain profitable sales.

Once a product is reaching the later phase of growth strong cash management is vital. This will involve emphasis on cost reduction, using capacity to its fullest, limiting expenditure on promotion, tighter credit control, and aiming to increase stockturn. Prices need to be stabilized or even raised. Less successful products should be pruned to free up capacity. The dual aim is to maintain market position and generate cash and capacity for investment in new products.

## The product portfolio

If the objective is to achieve profitability over a period of time then it is essential to review the product portfolio regularly, and to create an active policy for weeding out old declining products and for developing new products.

A strong share in a dynamic market results in growing sales, and the greater the volume produced the greater the market share. Often this results in lower costs per unit and higher margins in total than your competitors. There are a number factors which influence this:

- Better processes and design are brought about by constant improvements and experience.
- Production to greater capacity results in lower charges per unit for direct labour and overheads.
- Depreciation charges are spread over more units.
- Capital costs do not increase in direct proportion to output.
- Economies of scale in purchasing help create a lower cost per unit.

The first approach is to categorize your products. The Boston Consultancy Group has suggested four colourful but apt groups:

1. *Cash cows*. Products in this group will be well established leaders in a stable type of market. They continue to generate high cash levels without too much investment. The market is mature and may hold for a long period of time.
2. *Stars*. These are younger products which are showing a continuing increase in market share. They are more or less self-financing but will need further cash injection to help them grow further.
3. *Dogs*. These are products with little future, and which are draining cash (often described as 'managerial ego trips'). The market is static and growth rate is extremely slow.
4. *Wild cats*. Sometimes called 'question marks'. Products in this group have not yet achieved a dominant market position. The market segment is buoyant, and the chances of success are good but they are currently using up a lot of cash. Businesses cannot afford to carry more than a few wild cats.

In creating a portfolio the first aim is to identity and get rid of the dogs. There is little point in ploughing cash into markets with little or no growth. Cash cows are very desirable, and stars should be kept and pushed. Wild cats are also important in that the new stars will come from this generation.

- *The route of product development* is a cycle of new wild cats developing into stars, and eventually settling down as cash cows.

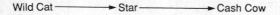

Wild Cat ⟶ Star ⟶ Cash Cow

- *The route of cash flow* is to use the cash generated by the cash cows to invest in the stars and in a limited number of wild cats

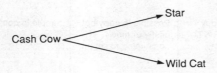

Cash Cow ⟨ Star / Wild Cat

Effective product portfolio management means being able to identify the category of a product and its relative position in the life cycle. This should make it easier to predict the shape and length of the life cycle in the future, and to forecast where it will be in, say, three years from now.

Where do the individual items in your product range fit in terms of life cycle and category? Can you identify reasons for any product decline, such as technical change, fashion trends, competition? Should these products be phased out, or are there good reasons, such as continuing satisfactory profit margins, to justify introducing new competitive effort? It is important to add that products do not rigidly 'fit' one of the four categories above. There are degrees of fit, and the solution or plan will vary accordingly.

## How strong is the product?

So far we have asked what influences customer choice, and how your products fared in the scale of satisfying customers' needs. It is time now to make an internal assessment of the product, and of any product policies your organization may have. How do people in the company view product design and quality?

Figure 3.2 outlines various aspects which should be discussed in detail. Each item will carry a different weighting according to the type of business. However, there is one thing of common importance – it is vital that all organizations can measure the profitability of each of its products, so that decisions can be made concerning product mix, promotion and purchasing. Each product demands a certain amount of finance, management time, selling costs, warehouse capacity and use of plant or machinery. A service will relate to several of these elements. The more you score in column 1 the stronger your position. The more you score in column 4 the

| 1 | 2 | 3 | 4 |
|---|---|---|---|
| *Product* Original in design, has a brand image, a specialist product. | An imitation of a leading brand. | A cheaper version | An average simple product. |
| *Ability to copy* Protected by patent, licence, copyright, registered design, registered trade mark. | Difficult to copy because of R & D time and costs. | Possible to copy but costly or time consuming to set up. | Simple to copy. |
| *Quality and specification* Always meets customer needs. | Well above customer needs. | Inclined to vary. | Often below the standard required. |
| *Profitability* All the products show a profit. | Some make profit, some break-even. | Some make profit, others break-even, some make a loss. | Cannot specify which products make profits or losses. |
| *New products* Policy to develop and introduce new products regularly. | Some new products – not on a regular basis. | Sometimes update old products when someone suggests it. | Same product since start-up. |
| *Packaging* Distinctive design, good quality materials. | Good design, functional. | Strong/functional design not considered important. | Basic but adequate. |

**Fig. 3.2**  Product strengths and weaknesses

more likely you can achieve growth by addressing the weaknesses, i.e. if you have done little to achieve 'USP' (a 'unique selling proposition') action should now be taken.

## Who are your competitors?

Your competitors' reactions to any marketing activity, especially at times when new products are launched or fresh markets attacked, are always a threat. You need to know who your competitors are, and keep a watchful eye on their behaviour. Existing competitors will be equally vigilant, and they will react accordingly in the areas of product, pricing and promotion.

Sudden or obvious success with a product or service will also draw in new competition from unknown sources who will be attracted by the apparently high margins, or the ease and speed with which products can be copied.

What you need to know and assess about the competition includes:

3

- Their names and their locations
- Company size, sales growth, profit growth
- Their market information
- Their traditional speed of reaction
- What they do better than you
- Their financial strength
- Size and diversity of product range
- Their promotional and sales literature
- What their weaknesses are.

---

At the end of several chapters there are activity lists and checklists which are designed to help in researching your business. Before you start, draw up an action plan which outlines your responses to the following:

- What areas are we going to research?
- Who will carry out each part?
- How much money is available?
- When is the information required?
- Who will use the resulting data?
- How will they use it?
- What shall we gain overall?

1. Gather monthly sales figures for the last two or three years of trading. Plot the figures on to a three or four year continuous graph (see Fig. 3.3). Draw a trend line through the graph then project this line on into the next year.

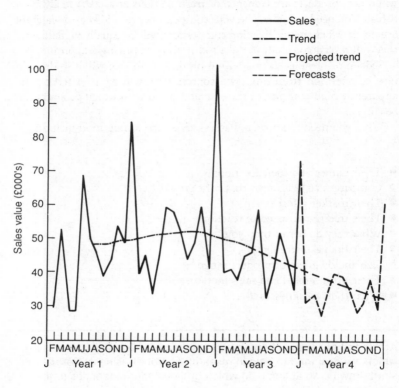

**Fig. 3.3** Graph of monthly sales showing projected trend

2. Plot each year's sales on to a twelve month graph, use different colours for each year (see Fig. 3.4). Note seasonal trends, problem periods, noticeable increases/decreases in trade. Look for differences in sales patterns. Where differences emerge find an explanation.

3. Using the sales ledger and/or other customer data, sort the information as follows:

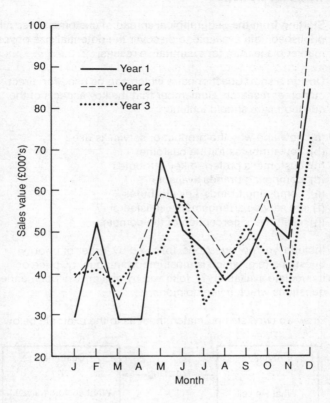

**Fig. 3.4**   Graph of monthly sales showing seasonal pattern

(a) The total number of customers, and the total sales value.
    Identify the key customers, measure them as a percentage of:
    (i) the total customer base, (ii) the total sales value.
(b) (i)   Divide customers into socio-economic groups.
    (ii)  Try other consumer groupings.
    (iii) Carry out the same exercise for key customers only.
(c) If you are in an industrial market, group your customers
    according to type and size of business.
(d) Group your customers according to geographical spread.
(e) Summarize the characteristics of (i) the customer, and (ii) the
    end user (this may be the same person).

4. Starting from the geographical spread of customers, use all the published data available to discover the potential size of your market place. Aim for quantitative results.

5. Design a short questionnaire which can be used for direct customer research. Remember that the key aspects of the questionnaire should include:

   (a) how and why the product or service is used
   (b) key attributes for the customer
   (c) customer's preferred key attributes
   (d) competing brands available
   (e) competing brands' key attributes
   (f) are service arrangements satisfactory?
   (g) customer's perception of the company.

   Include 'yes/no' questions, followed by 'order of priority' questions (e.g. which is most important: quality, price or immediate availability?), followed by one or two 'open ended' questions which invite opinions.

6. Draw up two lists and match them as in the example below.

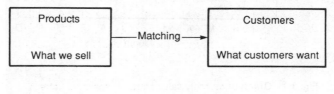

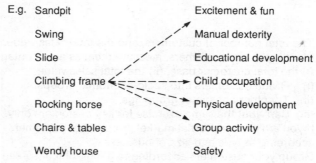

7. Draft life cycles for each of your key products. The time periods and incomes will differ from the example in the text.

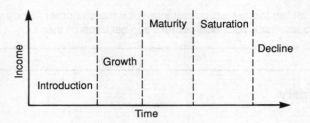

8. List your products under the following groupings:

| Cash cows | Stars | Wild cats | Dogs |
|-----------|-------|-----------|------|
|           |       |           |      |

9. List the strengths and weaknesses of each of your products/ services, looking carefully at design, quality, image, packaging, production and service.

10. (a)  Use *Yellow Pages* and other directories to list your competitors:

| Competitor name | Approximate turnover | Number of staff | Location | % share of local markets |
|-----------------|----------------------|-----------------|----------|--------------------------|
|                 |                      |                 |          |                          |
|                 |                      |                 |          |                          |

   (b)  Mark your territory on a map then plot the position of each competitor.
   (c)  Ask your local library to obtain the company accounts for those competitors which are limited companies. (There will be a small charge for this service.)
   (d)  Visit the premises of each competitor and try to glean as much information as possible about their style, products, staff and customers.

  (e) Gather all the promotional literature, price lists, etc., of as
       many competitors as possible.

11. List all the factors which will influence the customer to buy your
     product. Rank your competitors against each of these.

---

## Summary

Forward planning starts by setting personal and economic
objectives for the owner/manager and the firm as a whole.
     Start by seeking to establish where you are now and where you
want to be.
     The analysis and understanding of trends and buyer behaviour
in your existing market will help in identifying potential markets
and determining the direction of the company.
     Much information can be gained from the existing company
data about sales levels, frequency of purchase, value, etc.
     Employees and customers can provide first-hand information
on the strengths and weaknesses of products and services. This
can be sought by direct or postal questionnaire, informal or
telephone interview, and observation.
     There are a number of published sources of information such as
government publications and the trade press, which provide
information on tastes and trends, population, incomes, etc. Many
of these can be found in public libraries.
     All products have a life cycle of growth, maturity, and decline;
however, the rate varies and some products enjoy recycles.
     A product or service is seen by the customer as a problem-
solver – it solves his or her problems. Therefore it is important to
think of the products/services in terms of 'benefits to the
customer' rather than their physical attributes. Choice is
influenced by the presentation of the right benefits to each market
segment.
     Regular reviewing of the product portfolio is essential. The
nature of the product base will change as markets decline and new
products are introduced.
     Competition is a constant threat, especially at the growth stage
of a product, therefore vigilance is important.
     An important objective is to balance sales growth, cash flow
and risk.

# Checklist

---

1. How are decisions made about your product mix, specifications and style?
2. Does your company have a proliferation of products and markets?
3. Are your products costed?
4. How do you price your products? Is there pricing confusion?
5. Are your products what the market wants, or what you prefer to produce?
6. Have you lost opportunities for profit?
7. Is there a gap in the existing market for a new product?
8. Would a new product fill a gap in the existing product range?
9. Are there plans for new products at this moment?
10. Is it the policy to introduce regularly new products based on analysed customer needs?
11. Does your firm usually launch its new products *before* or *after* its competitors?
12. Is there a regular product progress review?
13. Do you know the contribution of each product?
14. Is packaging considered an important part of the marketing exercise?
15. Do staff feel committed to the firm's products?
16. Is your firm now stronger or weaker than the competition?

---

# 4 Do you have the resources?

Do you have the right staff? □ Do you have a good information system? □ Do you have the right supplies? □ Do you have the physical resources? □ The business environment □ Summary □ Checklist

The best laid plans are those based on a firm understanding of the company's capabilities and opportunities. So far you have identified the competition and examined customer profile and product characteristics. However, if you are going to formulate a plan for growth you will need to subject the organization to a thorough analysis, in order to isolate what you consider to be the strengths of the company, and to identify weaknesses or shortcomings.

The internal assessment will need to be carried out with complete frankness and objectivity. When it comes to looking closely at his or her own business the owner/manager is likely to have blind spots and needs to recognize this at the start. Managers and supervisors will also be somewhat reluctant when their own areas of responsibility are under scrutiny, so tact and intuition will prove useful tools.

In most small and medium sized firms the owner/manager seldom has access to information which gives a clear picture of the whole firm. Reports are usually limited to financial data, which is useful but not sufficient. Critical analysis is difficult, and it is best if the exercise is undertaken by a team, with the owner/manager acting as chairman. Those members of the team, who are the people ultimately responsible for implementing changes, would find it difficult to go through the process without gaining new insights and ideas to help plan more effectively for the future profitability of the firm.

Where possible, views and opinions should be sought from the widest range of staff. Such consultation will promote a sense of involvement and will help reduce resistance to change when new plans are introduced.

How does the business work from day to day? The manufacturer will be concerned with how the product is made, details of components, supplies, space, production capacity, and the amount of capital needed for additional operating costs. There are a number of elements which need close scrutiny, for example the need to achieve high levels of quality, reliable timing on delivery, and the avoidance of bottlenecks caused by such inefficiencies as unskilled staff or materials shortages.

The retailer might pay close attention to merchandise, shop decor, display, hours of opening, and the ability of staff to relate to customers. If you supply a service then you are concerned with what is involved in supplying that service, which might include finding materials, carrying out research, finding staff with the right skills, and having the ability to present and communicate.

## Do you have the right staff?

Small firms tend to be weak in the areas of organization and control. There is often a general lack of human resources in all areas, and especially in what could be termed 'non-productive' staff. Typically each manager has a wide spread of responsibilities ranging from production to sales. In the very small firm the owner/manager does everything – production, research, accounts – usually concentrating on the thing he or she is good at, while other aspects of the business suffer. On the other hand this very wide range of responsibilities undertaken by each individual often offers interest and variety, and usually generates good working relationships and a sense of team spirit.

Nevertheless, as the owner/manager you will aim to see that the talents and resources at your disposal are directed towards making money. With expansion comes the need for close examination of the qualities and characteristics of the people involved in the enterprise. Are they up to the tasks ahead of them?

The possible development of manager-led departments may involve recruiting specialist executives to help run the business. Unfortunately when the firm gets bigger, knowledge is more fragmented as new people take over separate functions. Those old informal systems for reviewing information will now be inadequate, and more formal approaches have to be introduced. Thus inevitably personal relationships between owner/managers and employees diminish.

Who are the people in your business? What are their particular skills and talents? What sort of qualities and characteristics dominate? You will need to assess the things that are good and moving the firm forward, and the areas where there are skills shortages or personnel issues which may be restraining growth. Sometimes if there is evidence that there are attitude or morale problems, better results can be gained by bringing in an outsider who can be completely objective.

## Are you a good manager?

As the business expands you will be faced with having to build a team, and learning to delegate some of the day-to-day authority. Becoming a manager in a more formal sense of the word will involve developing the skills of chairmanship and leadership. You will now have to encourage constructive thinking and participation from managers and staff alike. As the leader, your main tasks are centred around deciding what has to be done, selecting ways of achieving this, and ensuring that work is carried out efficiently. This could be summed up under three main headings:

- Setting objectives
- Planning
- Controlling.

In Chapter 13 we will look at the skills of leadership in greater detail. At this point we are concerned with discovering what skills are available, management and otherwise, and what skills are needed.

## Do you have a good information system?

All too often small businesses fail because they have not got sufficient administrative backup. Consequently, when an opportunity presents itself it is difficult to make decisions with any certainty that it is possible to follow them through. The administrative systems must grow with the firm, and be efficient enough for keeping accurate records and capturing the kind of information – such as sales, costs, funding, supplies, workload, etc. – needed for effective decision-making.

However, it is not necessary to change everything and to implement expensive new systems in order to introduce efficiency. But it is important to recognize needs as they arise. Are your administrative systems able to cope with your future plans? Should they be expanded?

If your method of reporting is a simple analysed cash book which is balanced monthly, then the time has come to expand the system. A growing business needs to know the cash position on a weekly basis, and sometimes on a daily basis. Every week there should be information on sales levels (especially the mixture of products sold), stock levels, out of stock items, orders outstanding and overdue deliveries.

Each month the reporting system should be sufficient to provide the following information:

- Analysis of sales and stocks by product groups.
- Aged analysis of debtors and creditors.
- Figures for updating the cash flow budget.
- A profit and loss account.
- Comparison of actual achievement with plans.
- Daily, weekly, monthly bank balance.

## Do you have the right supplies?

Materials and stocks often represent a major proportion of the total assets of a small business. Very large stock levels can reduce the profitability of a business by tying up a large proportion of the working capital. However, low stock levels can be even more costly. If merchandise is not available when customers are ready to buy, sales can be lost. Stock levels need to be constantly monitored to ensure that they do not become too large or too small, and that the right stock is being purchased.

A retail store, or merchandising company, buys stocks in a form ready to be sold without further processing or conversion. In contrast, a manufacturing company has three types of stocks – raw materials, work in progress and finished goods. Raw materials can include anything from unprocessed materials to technologically advanced components. Work in progress includes raw materials plus the labour and overhead costs incurred to date in converting the raw materials to finished goods.

Good stock management means maintaining an adequate stock to permit flexibility in production or sales, but which will not tie up an excessive amount of the company's funds. Many growing small businesses will look for opportunities to buy stocks in greater bulk at discounted prices. It must be noted that bulk purchase discounts are only worthwhile if the cost of borrowing the money to buy the extra stocks is *significantly* less than the discount obtained on its purchase.

In the case of stocks which can be purchased and delivered quickly, it is wise to reduce the quantities held; and in the case of slow moving items, mark down the price straight away in order to free up both storage space and funds, each of which has a measurable cost.

The purchase of materials and services is another area in which the principles of market research can be employed. The objective is to find a range of suppliers who can deliver the right quality, at the right time, at the right price, and to build good working relationships. The bigger the organization the more onerous the tasks of buying and managing stock. The following points should be considered:

- Regularly assess your suppliers for quality, delivery, price.
- Be constantly aware of alternative sources of supply.

- Aim to specify requirements and delivery dates in good time.
- Introduce a purchasing and stock control system.
- Take purchase discounts if they are worth significantly more than the company's costs of funds (i.e. cost of borrowing the money).
- Obtain staggered deliveries for merchandise on order instead of one large delivery.
- Identify and dispose of obsolete items.
- Mark-down prices on slow moving items.
- Increase security on merchandise susceptible to theft.

It is sometimes difficult to find supplies of specific materials, especially when the item is manufactured abroad. Your local information library should have UK and international directories, such as Kompass, which list names, addresses and telephone numbers of producers and consumer goods stockists. Small firms often find it impractical to finance the import of large container loads of any one material, therefore the practical answer is to find a UK stockist who will sell part loads or sample packs at a higher unit cost.

## Do you have the physical resources?

What degree of risk can the firm afford to take? Small firms have limited resources and this financial weakness is exposed when the business starts to grow.

Here we are concerned with looking at existing resources, and assessing their strengths and weaknesses with regard to plans for the future. Will the fixed assets need to be improved and updated? Describe the existing premises and their location. Measure their suitability for now and for the future. Will you need to move or seek additional premises; if so, when?

Itemize important plant and equipment. Have you got sufficient capacity? Consider what you need to expand, and the costs of new machinery. A point worth considering is the feasibility of subcontracting work as an alternative to capital investment, either as a short-term stop-gap or as a long-term feature.

Think about the time scales involved in carrying out repairs and improvements. If you need to move premises there will be staffing considerations, e.g. transfer of existing employees, availability of labour in the new locality, plus any extra staff and training which may be needed.

Look carefully at the costs involved, and consider how you propose to finance them. Finance is the subject of Chapters 7, 8 and 9.

## The business environment

'No man is an island' – the same can be said of a small business. It is appropriate at this point to mention outside decision-makers whose actions may have direct or indirect effects on the business's future. The interaction of governments, political influences, cultural changes and expectations, technological developments, sources of supply and competition, all play a large role in shaping and changing the path of business growth.

The greatest danger for any owner/manager is lack of awareness of change in these outside influences. Part of the assessment exercise involves looking at environmental factors and determining how these can be used positively as *opportunities*, or avoided if they constitute *threats*. These factors will be taken into consideration when drawing up the business objectives. The diagram in Fig. 4.1 illustrates the firm's position in its environment and the outside influences.

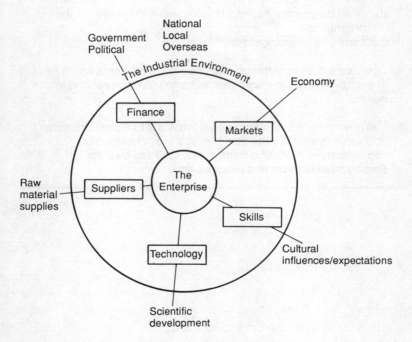

**Fig. 4.1** How the firm stands in the environment

1. Draw up an organizational chart of your company. Compare this with a key competitor.

2. List the main skills available in your organization.

3. Draw up a brief questionnaire on the following lines. Interview key members of staff on a formal or informal basis.

   (a) Has your job been outlined? Are you aware of your precise role?
   (b) Do you understand the roles of other members of staff, including the owner/manager?
   (c) Is there enough delegation?
   (d) Would more responsibility 'enrich' your job and lead to better working relationships?
   (e) Do you perceive a company image?
   (f) Do you understand costs, targets, budgets?
   (g) Does the organization foster/recognize talent?
   (h) Where would training provide extra skills or improve attitudes?
   (i) What do you see as the strengths and weaknesses of the organization?
   (j) Have you any suggestions?

4. Describe the administration and information systems which exist in your business. Do they measure up to your present and future needs?

5. Use government and other annual forecasts to assess the general economic climate for the next two years. There are many commentators, including trade press, bank reviews, the *Employment Gazette* and newspapers.

## Summary

A thorough internal assessment of strengths and weaknesses is a prerequisite to formulating plans for growth.

Where possible, seek staff involvement in the analysis. This will promote a sense of involvement and acceptance of change.

Start by analysing the talents and skills within the organization. Look for the strong features and establish future staff needs.

Procedures should become more formalized, and the owner/ manager will need to build a team to take on some of the managerial tasks.

The administrative system must grow with the business. This is the time to assess the existing systems, and to make decisions about present and future needs.

Sources of supplies need to be researched for quality, reliability, speed of delivery and price. It is advisable to find several suppliers, rather than rely on a key supplier.

Discounts on purchases should only be taken if the saving is significantly more than the cost of borrowing.

Small firms have limited resources. The capital needs may include an increase in fixed capital items such as vehicles and machinery, and an increase in working capital for stock and overheads.

The business grows and responds to environmental threats and opportunities.

4

## Checklist

---

1. Does everyone know their responsibilities?
2. Are the levels of management in the organization kept to a minimum?
3. Is the organization structure flexible enough to react to changing conditions?
4. Is there enough delegation of decision-making?
5. Are staff regularly appraised?
6. Is the management aware of the employees' full range of abilities and interests?
7. Are staff told of plans to make changes in advance?
8. Are your information systems adequate?
9. Is work organized in a logical way to avoid overlap and duplication?
10. Is your dispatch area cluttered with stock?
11. Does congestion often mean loss of stocks and materials, and difficulty in keeping records?
12. Are the premises large enough, and in a good safe condition?
13. Do you need new machinery and equipment?
14. Are there any noticeable changes in the environment which are affecting your business?

---

# 5 Drawing up the plan

What are your ambitions? □ How shall we achieve the objectives? □ How do we get there? □ Summary □ Checklist

A written marketing plan helps to make things happen, mostly because a number of people have been pushed into paying attention to the issues. What sort of business is required in five years' time? What are the considerations?

How far ahead might it be realistic to plan your business? On the whole, for most small and medium sized firms, it would be sensible to undertake detailed sales and tax planning, with associated budgets, for the next two years, and to plan and budget ahead for capital items five, and sometimes even more, years ahead. Considerations should include any likely effect from changes in the market place, the business, competitors, suppliers, etc., and plans will have to take account of scarcity of resources inside and outside the business.

The research undertaken in previous chapters will create a database from which you can draw information on the strengths and weaknesses of market related issues. Once you have identified market gaps and opportunities – also any external conditions which may affect the plans – the next stage involves setting realistic and achievable objectives for the major products and markets. This is a mandatory step in the planning process. It will ensure that a company knows what it is expected to accomplish.

## What are your ambitions?

Before you design your market plan give some time to your overall objectives, i.e. outline your ambitions. This will help set the scene by showing clearly the direction in which you wish to take the organization, and how far you intend to stretch the resources in order to achieve those objectives. They will also give a clear indication of cash and other resource requirements. However, if they are to be effectively put into action your ambitions must be compatible with existing strengths, and equally important, must not conflict with one another.

- *What is the nature of the business?* You should now have a clearer picture in answer to this question, which was raised in an earlier chapter.
- *Where do you want to be?* The review of the company's strengths and weaknesses will have indicated how the firm is best equipped to develop.
- *What are the personal objectives of the owner/manager?* This is a statement of the individual aspirations for growth by whatever means, whether it is to achieve wealth, have two factories, or to have personal contact with every customer, etc. it is vital that this question is given thoughtful consideration.
- *What are the areas in which success is vital to the firm?* The answers to this question are bound up with the owner/manager's personal objectives.

As far as possible the objectives should be quantifiable. They will be based on a knowledge of where we are now, i.e. the present market, and the current level of sales and profit margins, so it should be possible to put figures to the stated objectives. From these targets, cash and resource requirements can be outlined, and it should be possible to forecast future profit levels.

The examples below might represent the objectives for a particular small firm with three key products/services:

(a) *Increase* turnover by 20% in twelve months.

(b) *Increase* gross margins by 3% in twelve months.

(c) *Improve* cash flow. Clear overdraft by the end of six months.

(d) *Increase* sales to retail outlets in Scotland by 25% during the next nine months.

(e) Product X – mature market, *maintain* sales level for as long as possible; phase out when sales decline.

(f) Product X luxury model – *enter* in the same market as product X in three months time, aim for steady growth of 5% on product X sales.

(g) Product Y – *improve* market position by 15% increase in sales in twelve months.

(h) Product Z – *enter* in new market, aim for sales of £n which is a market share of x% in twelve months.

*Marketing objectives* can be based on four main categories (known as the Ansoff matrix), which are solely concerned with selling products to markets:

1. To sell EXISTING products in EXISTING markets.
2. To sell EXISTING products in NEW markets.

3. To sell NEW products in EXISTING markets.
4. To sell NEW products in NEW markets.

Any form of trade you undertake will follow one of these routes. The diagram in Fig. 5.1 illustrates the relationships.

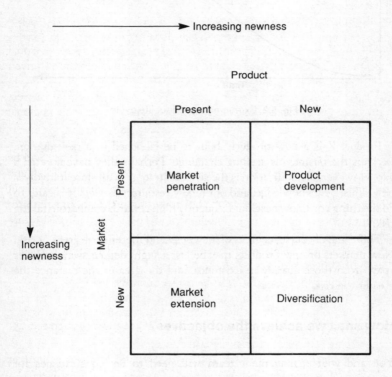

**Fig. 5.1** The Ansoff matrix

In the example objectives previously outlined, product X has reached a 'mature' situation in the product life cycle. It is generating good cash levels without too much expenditure, and could be termed a 'cash cow'. The firm wishes to continue with the product as long as demand can be maintained. The luxury model is to be introduced at an appropriate point in order to boost sales and prolong the life cycle (see Fig. 5.2). One of the problems is getting the timing right.

Product Y is already showing growth potential in attractive markets. The company aim is to penetrate the market even further. This approach to increasing profits and cash flow is the most cost effective and least risky, because they have knowledge and experience of the market.

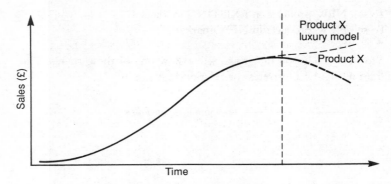

**Fig. 5.2** Extending a product life cycle

Product Z is a new product about to be launched in a new market. Perhaps the business is seeking challenge. Perhaps they have spotted a gap. However, diversification is the riskiest strategy of all since it involves new skills, new knowledge, and often new resources as well. It is safer to do the thing you know best, but frequently high rewards come from taking risk.

There are, of course, degrees of 'newness' and therefore degrees of risk. New markets or new products may be just a slight degree away, or poles apart from those already in existence, and the greater the distance the greater the risk.

## How shall we achieve the objectives?

You and your management team will need to design strategies for operating in each of the market segments you have identified. These strategies will form the basis upon which the detailed operating plans will be drawn up. The strategies and plans are designed for preparing the whole organization for increased activity brought about by seizing market opportunities.

Your marketing strategies will include elements commonly known as the 'four Ps': Product, Price, Place, Promotion.

1. *Product.* This involves making decisions on:
   - attributes which satisfy customer needs, such as design, quality, performance;
   - whether to expand or reduce the range;
   - the product mix;
   - branding.

2. *Price*. There are different approaches available for pricing products in different market segments. Decisions must be made on:
   - changing prices, offering discounts, credit periods;
   - entering the market with a high initial price, known as 'skimming';
   - entering the market with a low initial price, known as a 'penetration policy'.
3. *Place*:
   - This will include decisions on methods of distribution and selling, whether wholesaling, direct selling, retailing, agents, distributors.
   - You need to decide on the number of salesmen, agents, etc., and on their quality, style, delivery record, etc.
4. *Promotion*. This strategy decides how the business communicates with the market place. It will involve the choice of:
   - advertising – TV, radio, newspapers, magazines, etc.;
   - publicity material – brochures, leaflets, gifts, stationery, etc.
   - public relations exercises – press releases, promotions;
   - exhibitions, trade fairs, etc.

5

The decisions on how you will tackle each market segment will include different combinations of the elements outlined above. Formulating marketing strategies is the most difficult part of the process since every aspect of the decision has an effect on all parts of the business. Each aspect is interlinked so the jigsaw has to be broken and reassembled as often as it takes to arrive at a set of strategies which will 'fit'. Therefore the overall task is to design feasible strategies around which management will be able to plan and coordinate operating activities.

## How do we get there?

Having decided on which strategies to adopt the question always arises – how should we get there? The final part of the planning, known as the marketing plan, is a very detailed set of plans which lay out how the strategies should be put into action for every section of the business that is affected: the putting together of the jigsaw. The plans will take account of scarcity of resources such as cash, premises, machinery, labour and management. Figure 5.3 sums up the processes involved in arriving at a final marketing plan.

Research takes time, effort and money, but without it you will be unable to make informed decisions. If the marketing plan is developed from good information you should be better able to forecast sales, which in turn will provide a basis for predicting the financial viability of your growth plans.

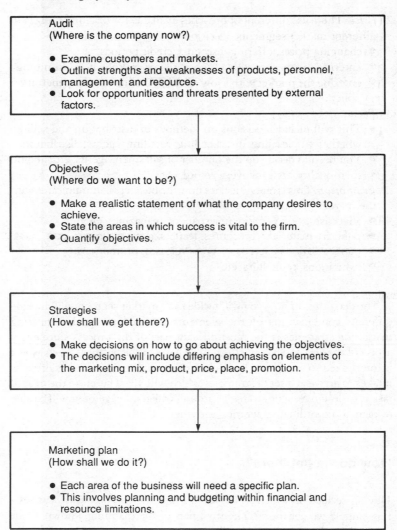

**Fig. 5.3** The planning processes

Forecasting sales is therefore dependent on all the areas discussed in previous chapters. These include:

- Knowing about past performance of the product or service, and of similar products.

- Understanding your customers' needs, and knowing about opportunities which exist.
- Knowing how well your business can meet the challenge.
- Trade information from trade associations, suppliers and other sources.
- Trends of fashion.
- The strengths and weaknesses of the competition.
- Intuition and instinct.
- Examining and assessing external factors such as inflation, interest rates, legislation.

## Planning the growth

You are now at the start of the growth planning stage. Every business will have different problems, different products, different markets. It is outside the scope of this book to examine every aspect of planning for each specific business. However, there are many topics related to managing growth that are common to all businesses. The following chapters seek to highlight and discuss these areas.

5

---

1. The owner/manager must now decide on his or her own objectives for planning growth. Make a list of the benefits you are seeking for yourself, your staff, and your business.

   Refine this list by removing those aspirations which are unlikely, incompatible or probably unachievable.

2. As a team, decide on the company's *broad objectives*. They should be based on what you know about the firm's needs and the market's needs.

3. Spend considerable time refining these objectives and creating sub-objectives, until it is possible to express many of them in quantifiable terms:

| Objective | Target | Percentage | Time scale |
|-----------|--------|------------|------------|
|           |        |            |            |
|           |        |            |            |
|           |        |            |            |

4. Take each objective and decide on the best ways in which you might achieve it:

| Objective or sub-objective | Strategy – changes in: | | | |
|---|---|---|---|---|
| | Product | Promotion | Price | Place |
| 1. 2. 3. etc. | | | | |

5. Design detailed plans for the changes indicated. This must inevitably lead to planning resource needs, sales forecasting, cash flow and projected profit and loss account.

## Summary

Put your plans in writing. This will serve to concentrate thinking and generate commitment.

Small businesses should plan in depth for the next three years, and consider longer-scale planning for capital items. Planning is not just a once-a-year exercise. All plans should be regularly monitored, updated and referred to as working documents.

Previous research into company strengths and weaknesses and environmental opportunities and threats provides the basis for planning.

Marketing plans must be based upon the clearly stated objectives of the company, and the personal objectives of the owner/manager.

Strategies for achieving objectives are based on elements of the 'four Ps': product, price, place, promotion.

The market plan is a detailed set of plans designed for putting strategies into action.

## Checklist

1. Are you preoccupied with short-term thinking?
2. Do you plan ahead?
3. Is planning a once-a-year ritual?
4. Do your plans consist largely of numbers, e.g. target turnover, target profits (gained by adding 10% on last year's figures)?
5. Is planning delegated to a planner?

# 6 Reaching a wider market

The communication process □ The promotional budget □ Planning the promotional mix □ Advertising □ Sales promotion □ Public relations □ Press relations □ The sales force □ Channels of distribution

Now that you have carried out the research and decided on the product mix and the market segment, the next stage is to draw up a plan of action showing how you intend to communicate with your customers. The precise nature of this challenge will depend upon a number of factors, including whether you sell to domestic consumers or trade customers. If the target market has been defined well you should know where the customers are, what they read, and where they congregate.

This chapter looks at the various methods of communication which are available to a small firm to enable you to consider and design the appropriate sales/promotion package for the business and its products. The outcome will be based on a plan for achieving the marketing objectives which have now been defined.

A business which is already operating in the market place will have discovered various ways and means of promoting its products. These methods will now need to be evaluated as part of the planning exercise. Many small firms do not advertise because the word of mouth network has been sufficient to generate enough work to keep the business fully extended. Often these firms arrive at the growth stage suspicious of promotion, or at least being uncertain of its value. However, a firm which has undertaken significant investment in growth must now take the business of reaching a wider market very seriously.

Promotion is a form of communication between the firm and others, notably existing and potential customers. Successful promotion is based on an understanding of the communication process. Clever promotional activity is capable of turning an ordinary product into a winner. Indeed, large companies have sometimes been able to cause ordinary 'me too' products to become household necessities. The lesson for the owner/manager is that 'better than average' promotion may enable the business to outscore its competitors and might at times be more important than differences in the product.

## The communication process

The communication process means promoting the firm or its products to customers and to others such as staff, shareholders and suppliers. You can deliver the message by a direct face-to-face approach, or use a mixture of indirect methods, changing the emphasis according to the audience. Generally it is felt that a good combination of direct and indirect methods will achieve the best results. For the small firm it is a question of devizing the most cost-effective approach.

Direct methods include:

- Employing sales people.
- Exhibiting at trade or consumer exhibitions and fairs.
- Giving in-store demonstrations.

Indirect methods include:

- Advertising – press, TV, radio, billboards, posters, etc.
- Brochures and leaflets about the company and the products.
- Public relations – news stories, features, video tapes, conferences, facility visits from press, etc., internal magazines, news sheets.
- Promotions – special events.

Before we can determine the promotional mix, we must determine who the intended recipient of the message is. Having carried out market research you will have an understanding of the buying processes of certain key customers. For instance, in an industrial market there are likely to be several influencers in the buying decision, therefore the message needs to convey several aspects of the product's properties so that all the influencers may be convinced that your product is the one they most need.

The overall objective of market communication is to gain greater profitability through the generation of sales, the means of achieving which can range from extremely subtle 'image building' to making bold and direct statements. Therefore in deciding on promotional activity you will need to think about the objectives of the message and then design the method and style accordingly. For instance, you may wish to:

- Create awareness of the product or service.
- Try to develop a 'brand', or create customer loyalty.
- Inform customers of the benefits of the product.
- Launch a new product and/or enlarge the customer base.
- Create a company image, or improve the company's credibility.
- Deter the competition, i.e. defensive promotion.

For all communication decisions it is important to consider the following set of questions.

- What are we trying to achieve?
- What is the target audience?
- What is the message?
- Which media should be used?
- What will it cost?
- How can we get feedback?

## The promotional budget

How much should you spend on advertising and promotion? The cash flow will dictate this to some extent. Many companies decide in advance on how much they can afford, and this is often based on allocating a fixed percentage of sales income, say 3 to 5 per cent of last year's turnover. This method does have its drawbacks: (a) the lower the turnover the less there is to spend and (b) it promotes the attitude that advertising and promotion is an expense rather than an investment in the future of the company.

It is far better to work out the promotional effort needed to fulfil your objectives and then cost it out, rather than work on the basis of what you can afford. You will be constrained ultimately by the cash flow, but at least you will have allowed space for some strategic thinking. Look upon your promotion as an investment which will pay off in sales, and budget for it as you would for any other financial commitment. As such you will expect and look for a return on that investment.

To some extent the amount spent must be related to your specific objectives. The larger the desired increase in turnover the further you may have to spread your message. If you wish to export for the first time then you will experience high initial promotion costs. Also, costs will vary according to the industry you are in and whether you are selling to an industry consisting of a small number of large firms or a highly fragmented market. In some consumer markets, e.g. cosmetics, promotion is among the most significant of all costs, but your business promotion costs should not be a high proportion of the turnover.

The budget must be apportioned between those promotional activities which have been chosen as the most appropriate for the company. Every pound spent on advertising is a pound less for some other aspect of promotion, thus, like all other costs, they must be monitored so that the budget and its apportionment can be kept under review. With the support of a good information system the business should ultimately be able to move to a situation where the optimum promotional budget can be determined, and its allocation can be fine tuned. It is useful to establish a budget policy, and in order to do this you will need to get as much of the information system as possible in place before the promotional effort is launched.

A business cannot afford to spend money on an advertising campaign without knowing how effective it is. Test the campaign over a short period and look at the results. Try various media to find the most cost-effective in terms of expense and effort. Involve your staff in monitoring the results. Make sure they give customers a good reception and have them ask for feedback; this applies to the switchboard, enquiry desk, salespeople and other staff who have contact with customers.

## Planning the promotional mix

The action plan will consist of some combination of the wide range of activities open to you even as a small firm. This means deciding on how to get the message to the carefully chosen destination group. All means available to the business for achieving this deserve close attention, but here we concentrate on those means that are capable of being widely used by all small firms.

## Advertising

Most small businesses are familiar with placing advertisements in their local newspaper, but how many consider whether this is the right medium, or even consider other local media for the purpose? Advertising helps keep your name and the advantages of the product or service in front of the customers, and need not be a hit or miss affair. One question you will ask is, '*Will it work?*'. The answer is very much defined by how you judge its success. If there is a direct increase in sales then the advertisement can be said to have worked. On the other hand, in a highly competitive situation advertisements may work by maintaining sales levels which may otherwise have declined due to promotion by the competition. If your product is in a declining market then advertising may help slow down the decline.

The level of success in the two latter examples is not easy to measure, but your market research will have highlighted the prevailing conditions and it may be possible to predict what would have happened had you not defended your position or prolonged the life-cycle. Advertising will also make others aware who were not so previously, and the outcome of this, hopefully increased sales, may not occur until some time after the event, which means that there is probably an unmeasurable element of success.

In designing an advertisement we need to define our objectives carefully, since the message we deliver will flow from them. Market research is aimed at discovering the size of the targeted market segment and the characteristics of the customers within that segment. It is also concerned with the characteristics of the products, how they are perceived, and how well they meet customer needs. For example, in taking a new product into the market, or an existing product into a new market segment, the objective will be to raise awareness of both the company and the product in the first instance.

The advertising will be based on taking the customers through a process in stages, starting from being unaware of the product and the company name. The next stage is to promote the product so that the potential customer understands its uses, likes its appearance and begins to appreciate all the product differentials, until finally the desire to buy moves the customer to actually purchase. If we look at this as a set of steps then the aim is to move potential customers from their current stance to a step higher up the ladder. As they reach the decision they weigh up the information provided, and finally (hopefully) decide to buy.

On the other hand, the advertising objective may be to promote an existing product in an existing market, that is, to aim at the current users of our product, users of other similar products, or past users of the product. There will also be non-users in this category. The message would carry a number of objectives, such as:

- informing non-users
- persuading all users that our product has better characteristics
- reminding past customers of its uses
- congratulating current users of our products (helps create a 'brand')
- giving it a specific identity which relates to the user group.

Launching a new product or opening a new outlet often calls for advertising that creates an impact. This may mean large displays and/or advertisements, backed up by radio or direct mail, over a short period. Your budget is not going to enable you to sustain this effort. It may mean that you should consider how you spread your promotion allowance over the budget period. To make the necessary impact, 'front-loading' may be necessary. Once the company name or that of the product has been circulated, low cost but frequent advertising can follow. For some products increasing sales may simply mean stepping up the frequency of low cost advertising only. Sometimes 'little and often' beats the occasional big splash.

## Do you intend to grow regionally or nationally?

If the business is aiming for growth within a region or locality, you will not usually wish to send messages all over the country. However, you may need to advertise in a specialist national journal in order to reach industrial specialists. The target market may be heavily concentrated in one region, or it may be a more widely dispersed industry where there are sufficient recipients within your own target area to justify a national approach, especially if it is based on low cost, small advertisements, and the alternative methods of reaching your target group are more expensive. Careful study of the circulation of the journal, the cost of advertising, and the geographic distribution of the industry will pay dividends.

When offering a local service to consumers or the business community the choice of promotion narrows down to the local media. If the newspaper has to be paid for then it is likely to be read (and not just by its purchaser). Freely issued papers and journals are more likely to be discarded, but against that, their distribution is quite well controlled.

When the product or service is needed in a variety of different industries you will have to decide on whether to use publications circulated over a wide range of businesses or concentrate the advertising effort into those journals addressed to a single industry. Similarly, there are general and specialist consumer magazines. In all cases circulation and readership figures and costs should be considered in the light of the advertising objectives and the cash flow. One approach could entail joint advertising; for instance, retailers often combine with their suppliers and customers in joint advertising features which are sometimes backed by editorial comment.

## Designing the advertisement

The target market is a prime consideration when designing the style and content of an advertisement. For example, the objectives, to persuade, sell, inform or maintain customer loyalty, may be the same for consumer and industrial markets but the copy and the style will be very different. Industrial advertising is often technically informative since it is aimed at people who will be looking for product differentials in technical fields. Consumer advertising uses simple language and keeps technical information to a minimum.

The copy and artwork must be of high quality otherwise the advertisement will not succeed. It is important to obtain feedback from the recipients; however, if the copy is poor, the response is likely to be noncommittal; i.e. the customer will be unable to identify why the advertisement did not work. Unfortunately, in the absence of feedback it is possible to reach the wrong conclusions as to the viability of the exercise.

The business may have the ability to prepare its own copy, but as the company expands and the demands upon time increase, it may be beneficial to entrust the work to a good advertising agent who comes well recommended. Much depends on the business's stage of growth, capability, and ability to substitute time for money. If writing your own copy consider the following:

- Make your advertisement different, even unconventional.
- Keep the copy to a minimum.
- Make use of space and do not overload the advertisement with too much detail.
- State the message clearly, sticking to one theme that is consistent with the overall promotion plan.
- Promote the benefits of your product or service rather than your corporate identity (which is something that may follow at a later stage).

## Direct mail and direct response advertising

These are specialized forms of advertising. Direct response may involve the supply of a catalogue or other form of sales literature which invites the customer to respond by placing an order through the post. Alternatively, customers may be invited to respond to newspaper or other media advertisements which ask them to buy 'off the page'. The product must be suitable for such advertising, and you will have an advantage if you have a good mailing list.

Direct mail is the fastest growing major advertising medium. It means that your message is delivered directly to the potential customer, thus eliminating intermediaries and moving the company closer to the market. The whole transaction takes place through the post and from the response the advertiser can build up a mailing list for future use.

For businesses whose customer lists are inadequate, there are companies who deal in selling classified mailing lists which contain the names and addresses of the type of customer you have identified. If you are selling to the consumer market and cannot find a suitable list, then the Consumer Locations System (CLS) could be considered. CLS uses two major sets of research data to identify ACORN types (ACORN is a classification system) on the electoral register. From this a list of your requested ACORN types can be extracted. Further details on CLS can be obtained from the Direct Mail Sales Bureau, Floral Street, London WC2E 9RR. The Post Office publishes several books on different aspects of direct mail. For details contact The Post Office Direct Mail Section, Room GO4, 22–25 Finsbury Square, London EC2B 2QQ.

## Sales promotion

The term 'sales promotion' embraces a number of short-term activities aimed at achieving specific tasks. For example, a company which has slow moving stock may undertake a promotional exercise for the purpose of releasing cash and making space available for new stock. Most sales promotion activities are concerned with time and time-limits, i.e. buying now, sooner, faster, before certain dates. They will offer benefits other than those classed as product differentials. The benefits could include gifts, commissions, extended guarantees, etc.

The type of promotion undertaken must be strictly in line with the overall objectives sought. Rather than offering a one-off gimmick, make the exercise fit the strategy for developing company image, so that it helps form the bond with the customer. Promotional schemes can and should be used as flexible and effective marketing tools, in both consumer and industrial markets.

There are many kinds of sales promotion. For example, in the consumer market there are cash incentives such as special purchases, price reductions, or 'money-off' vouchers. Often the benefit is related to free goods, 'buy one, get one free', gifts and trade-ins. In the service industry the promotion can take the form of exhibitions and displays, offering extra guarantees, inviting people to join in, and special events. In the industrial and trade markets, companies have developed schemes which include delayed invoicing, training schemes, gifts, competitions, free trials, trade-in offers, extended credit, etc.

When the objective is to undertake promotional activity to help launch a new product, then all the preparation must be geared towards a specific date. Customers, existing and potential, will have to be informed: this probably means expenditure on brochures, leaflets, advertising, and telephone communication. Mundane but necessary information for staff, such as price lists, order forms and offer summaries, must be prepared. Staff have to be briefed and trained as to their role, i.e. sales, support staff, administration, collecting data and feedback. A means of assessment should be decided on at the beginning so that the promotion can be properly evaluated.

Exhibitions provide another sales promotion opportunity. The cost of a major national or trade exhibition can be high, but if it draws in the buyers and decision-makers it could still be cost effective for small firms. The importance of making those contacts, all within a short period of time, and having the chance to show all of the products to a buyer who has come especially to see them, can be weighed against how much it would cost to make the same contacts by alternative means.

Exhibitions may be an important first step if you wish to export. There are also localized and lower cost exhibition opportunities such as those arranged by small business clubs, local authorities' economic development units, etc. Those who exhibit need to make sure that they invite the right people to visit. The promise of hospitality usually helps. Watch the local press and trade publications for exhibition opportunities, and learn something of the track records of these events from others. A comprehensive guide to forthcoming exhibitions is published in the *Exhibition Monthly* by the London Bureau, 266 Kirkdale, Sydenham, London SE26 4RZ (ph. (01) 778 2288). Your local college or Chamber of Commerce will also have information on short training courses for exhibitors. It is worth attending such a course with key staff, so that you can all assess the value of exhibitions and how to prepare for them.

## Public relations

The Institute of Public Relations describes PR as 'the deliberate, planned and sustained effort to establish and maintain understanding between an organization and its public'. In other words, public relations is an ongoing publicity effort which is based around building up a company image. It is a two-way communications process between the company and the recipients, who might include the public, shareholders, staff and suppliers. The techniques used will vary to match different situations and must be closely monitored.

Many small firms make effective use of calendars, diaries, beer mats, coasters, pens and other promotion gifts. The hope is that the recipient will keep the gift on his or her desk or close at hand, so that the company name and telephone number is readily obvious at an opportune moment. Something different, such as a personalised golf brolly, may be appropriate for a small number of key customers.

Competitions provide a useful means of building up a customer list and might be combined with market research. Offering a prize will attract people into the draw, in return they give their names and addresses and probably answer a short questionnaire. The prize may be something that is cheap for the company to give but is highly regarded by the customers. For example, you may have one child's tricycle left out of your stock of 100 and it refuses to move. It will be valued at full retail price by competition entrants, but to you the cost is trade price. Asking a local personality to present the prize will probably gain you free publicity in the local press. There are many variations on this theme open to small firms.

Businesses operating on a local basis frequently become involved with sponsorship of local activities. By providing shirts for a football team, or a venue or trophies for an event (especially when it is related in some way to the activities of the business) a company can build up a good relationship and image with the local community.

Hospitality events coupled with a new product launch or 'celebrations' can always be used to good advantage. Invitations sent out to key customers and suppliers, and to prominent members of the business community, will help to promote the company image and will provide an opportunity to display and demonstrate the product.

## Company image

Companies like Sainsburys and Marks and Spencers have a corporate image which means that they present a consistent face and style to the world. How far do you need to go in this direction?

It is appropriate to take steps to adopt a style that influences the perceptions people have of your business. The way you present your letter-heads or answer the telephone may seem less significant in relation to the total effort but it could be the factor by which a potential customer makes a decision. The professional image presented is often the deciding factor which allows a business to score over the competition. Take special care in the design of stationery, business cards, brochures, delivery vans, your reception area and anything else of a visible or communications nature. You should, as a minimum, have consistency in the area of printed material and colours. Develop a consistent print style and logo that appears on all vehicles, advertisements and stationery, thus building a recognizable identity.

## Press relations

Your plans for growth may present an opportunity for you to cultivate good press relations. Newspapers are still the most important source of local news, and a well-written story about some aspect of your business is of interest to local readers, especially if 'people' are highly featured.

Journalists and editors are always in the market for a good story. Story lines should not be difficult to find. Perhaps growth for your company means a new invention, an increased labour force, new premises, or a significant new contract or export order. When writing the press release keep in mind that articles are often only scanned and many stories are not read beyond the first paragraph, so try to summarize the entire story at the start.

Once your business features in the press look for reasons to reappear there as often as possible. Be alert to the possibilities, e.g. your 10,000th product, your charity run, an achievement or experience of a member of your staff, a visit by a special customer, etc. Photographs are always welcome to the press. Talk to the editors and find out just what they want. In one sense you are gaining free publicity, but remember that there is a little time involved and, as your business grows, you may decide to hand over the task to a public relations consultant.

An example of taking an opportunity: a local company had a young salesman in need of a second-hand bicycle so that he could deliver the firm's products more easily. A small 'wanted' advertisement was inserted in the local paper with the employer's name attached. The editor was persuaded by the business owner to make a story-line out of the salesman's dilemma. When the response for a bicycle came in, the newspaper was delighted to use the story as an example that their advertising worked – they even had a photographer on hand when the bicycle was handed over.

## The sales force

With expansion comes the increasing need to communicate with the market in a variety of ways. In a small firm the owner/manager often wears the hat of chief salesperson. As the business grows, more salespeople are employed and the organization is carved up either by territory, by product, or by customer type. It is not uncommon for the owner/manager to have difficulty in relinquishing key customers who can be scattered over the territories of the other salespeople.

At this point it is necessary to review the size and calibre of the sales force against the size and type of the business, and to draw up a sales plan which is based on the company's marketing objectives. What is the workload of the current salespeople? Do they undertake tasks, such as debt collection, which could be transferred to administration? Are there too many/too few salespeople for the size of the customer base? Will there be sufficient in six months' time?

You will need to work out with the sales team what could be expected of one salesperson per day in terms of number of calls, travel time, breaks, etc., when travelling within a certain radius. This will provide a basis for setting sales targets.

The sales force should be involved in providing information and suggestions for the construction of the marketing plan, so that they will understand the market segment aimed for, the characteristics and needs of the customers, the pricing policy, and the forecast sales, i.e. their targets. They should also be thoroughly versed in the properties and qualities of the products, and how these are designed to meet customer needs.

Another route to expansion lies in establishing representation by way of sales agents. This is most appropriate when you cannot afford your own sales force and can identify agents well connected in your field.

The sales plan will include setting up suitable administration systems for recording all the results of the selling effort, such as orders, enquiries, complaints, feedback on customers' likes and dislikes, changes in taste, changes in buying patterns, etc.

## Channels of distribution

Does reaching a wider market mean changing or extending your channels of distribution? The last stage in the marketing process is distribution, (which in terms of the 'four P's' is Place). Unfortunately, too many firms think of this merely in terms of delivery, when the real aim is to get the products in the right form to the right place at the right time.

In recent years many changes have occurred in the channels of distribution, especially with consumer goods. The key for many small firms could be finding the right middlemen. Some firms limit their growth prospects by clinging to the belief that middlemen should be eliminated, or by resenting the mark-ups they will apply. Some firms can expand and market directly (perhaps by mail order techniques), but growth is the time to reappraise attitudes as well as channels of distribution.

### What opportunities are presented by retail or wholesale outlets?

Can you take advantage of some of the changes that have taken place in recent years? For instance, petrol companies now pay careful attention to their forecourt shops and see them as being one of the means whereby they attract trade to their pumps and maximize selling opportunities. If your product fits the range of goods sold in such locations then you will find that the forecourt operators can give you decisions and information. There are also wholesale firms which specialize in supplying these outlets. In this case you have to set against the lower mark-up you get from a wholesaler the savings in time and administration resulting from a smaller number of larger customers. Petrol companies publish excellent in-house journals that will give you valuable information and help you decide about these as channels of distribution.

Newsagents are also forever expanding their product range, and many chemists shops have acquired a 'mini-market' appearance. If your business is a small company producing toys, clothing (boutiques might suit you), or household furniture, the choice of distribution channels will be wide, but not necessarily easy.

The owner/manager needs to work out the advantages of retail or wholesale outlets when compared with direct sales. If using outlets is profitable, a decision has to be made on which of them best fits the company's growth objectives in terms of profitability and stability. A company which chooses retail as a channel of distribution needs to think about point of sale material. If the right outlets are selected then the business can probably economize on advertising but boost sales by providing display cards, racks and dispensers. One form of retail outlet unlikely to accept a product unless there is large expenditure on advertising is the national supermarket chain. Before accepting the product they are likely to want to know how much is going to be spent on promotion. In this context promotion could well mean a national campaign beyond the means of small firms. Supermarkets are effectively order-takers who leave much of the promotion to the manufacturers.

## If you are selling to industry, have you reviewed your channels of distribution?

A business selling products or materials to industry will have fewer end-customers and may be dealing with them directly through the sales force or sales agent. However, there are occasions when distribution can take place through a wholesaler. It is really a question of economics, i.e. doing your sums. If the wholesale route is chosen the owner/manager can work with the wholesaler and monitor his or her performance.

In any event, whether you are in the consumer or industrial market, you have to consider the benefits sought by the middleman as well as those sought by the end-user. One aspect all middlemen will be seeking is efficient distribution in the physical and practical sense.

## Do you have your delivery act together?

Unfortunately, many firms put all of their previous effort at risk by treating delivery as a Cinderella activity. Marketing has to be seen as relating to all aspects of the business. Deliveries must be made on time. This might almost be your USP, arrived at as a result of having discovered the laxities of your competitors. Life in business, as elsewhere, is about expectations.

Sadly, small firms, overjoyed at receiving the order, may promise unrealistic delivery dates. It is better to provide a margin of safety and acquire a reputation for living up to delivery dates. If you promise six weeks and deliver in six, you will be thought more of than if you had promised four and delivered in six weeks.

Despite all your precautions however, there may be occasions when things go wrong. Sometimes, for instance, the business is let down by its own suppliers. In such a case the waiting customer should be informed immediately. Avoid the temptation of labelling everything as urgent in order to drive the staff. Such a label will quickly become meaningless. It is all too easy to blame late delivery on the rail or other transport system you have chosen to use. It is little consolation to the customer or middleman that you are not very good at selecting the right form of transport to help meet the requirement.

The choice of transport is quite wide. Your own drivers are a part of your marketing package, and this has implications in terms of their reliability, courtesy, tact and appearance. They are also valuable sources of information. Perhaps by discreet observation they will be able to tell which of your competitors are delivering to your customers. They may also learn something of how the customer perceives your image *and* that of your competitors.

6

## Summary

Having defined the market segment it is now necessary to show
how we intend to communicate with our customers. Seek to
build on and add to methods already in use. The promotional mix
will consist of a wide range of activities.

The communication process means promoting the company
and its products to existing and potential customers, staff,
shareholders, and suppliers. It can be carried out by a number of
direct and indirect methods. Any forms of communication must
be based on an objective such as creating awareness or brand
loyalty. We must ask ourselves what the target audience is, and
which media should be used.

A promotional budget should be looked upon as an investment
in the future which should pay off, rather than as an additional
expense.

Advertising is an important aspect of promotion. The wording,
the style, the media chosen, can be used for any objective, from
raising awareness of new products to regenerating sales of
existing ones, and for promotion in industrial markets. The
design, style and copy for an advertisement are prime
considerations. In industrial markets the advertisement seeks to
inform the customer about technical aspects.

Direct mail and direct response advertising is a fast growing
advertising medium. It delivers the message directly to the
potential customer, thus moving the company closer to the
market.

Sales promotion covers a number of activities aimed at
achieving fast response sales, for example, 'money-off' coupons
and trade-ins.

Exhibitions are expensive, however they may prove cost
effective in the long run.

Public relations are ongoing exercises undertaken by the
business, which will help maintain understanding between the
company and its customers and suppliers. This can be achieved by
hospitality, competitions, gifts, etc.

Press relations can afford the company excellent publicity,
much of this can be free or relatively cheap in the early stages.
Local journalists are always looking for good 'people' stories.

You will find details of all media in *British Rate and Data*
(BRAD), which is held in all main libraries. It gives advertising

rates, circulation and contacts for every magazine, radio station and newspaper currently available in the UK. Similar information can be found in *Hollis Press and Public Relations Annual* and *Benn's Media Directory*.

## Checklist

1. Have you laid down objectives upon which to base a planned promotion campaign?
2. Do you know which methods of advertising are most appropriate for your business?
3. Do you monitor the effectiveness of your advertisement in generating enquiries?
4. Do you monitor the extent to which enquiries are converted into sales? As a result do you know how cost-effective your advertisements are?
5. Do you ensure that your sales promotion is 'targeted'?
6. How does your promotional mix compare with that of your closest competitors?
7. How do other people view the quality of your sales literature and other promotional material?
8. When were you last featured in the press, or on radio or TV?
9. How often do you look around for a good story-line that will earn you free publicity?
10. Do you foster good relations inside your firm?
11. Do you keep your staff well-informed?
12. Does your sales force have total awareness of specific sales objectives?
13. Do you ensure that any sales targets are agreed with the sales people concerned?
14. Do you or your salespeople plan their routes and routines?
15. Do you monitor the activities and the performance of your sales force?
16. Are there experienced agents in your field willing to promote your product? What terms can you negotiate with these agents?
17. Do you have, or can you obtain, a sound mailing list?
18. Are you aware of the Mail Order Protection Scheme and media regulations?

# 7 Pricing for profits

Cost-plus pricing □ Market-based pricing □ Are you making a profit? □ How does the buyer decide? □ Summary □ Checklist

Trying to decide on the price for a new product is one of the most important and difficult tasks facing the owner/manager. At this point you may need to review your general pricing policies in the light of your proposed expansion. Your pricing decisions will become part of the plan designed for achieving the objectives you have outlined, e.g. target profits, launching new products, gaining a bigger share of the market.

In theory, pricing procedure is aimed at finding the 'right price' which will satisfy the customers' needs for value, and provide an acceptable contribution to the business. It is therefore a vital element of the marketing mix. There are several approaches used for deciding on price.

## Cost-plus pricing

This is one of the most commonly used methods. Basically it means finding the costs for materials and labour, then adding a share of the overheads and a further percentage for profit.

For a one-product firm which has easily identifiable costs this may seem very logical. The fixed overheads are simply shared over the number of units produced, and the variable costs (labour and materials) are added. The more units there are produced the cheaper the cost per unit. The graph in Fig. 7.1 illustrates this.

However, in a business where there are a number of products the headache starts when you try to find a basis for allocating fixed costs to units produced, because there are at least six 'costing' methods which can be used, and each one will provide a different answer. For example, *labour hours* may be the criteria for allocation: product A uses three labour hours, and product B uses two labour hours, so fixed costs are allocated on a ratio of 3 : 2. Alternatively *machine hours* could be the base: product A uses two machine hours and product B uses three machine hours, so the fixed costs are allocated on a ratio of 2 : 3. There are now two different sets of costs for the same products.

The results achieved by applying different methods of cost spreading to a bigger range of products are even more unsatisfactory. Nevertheless this

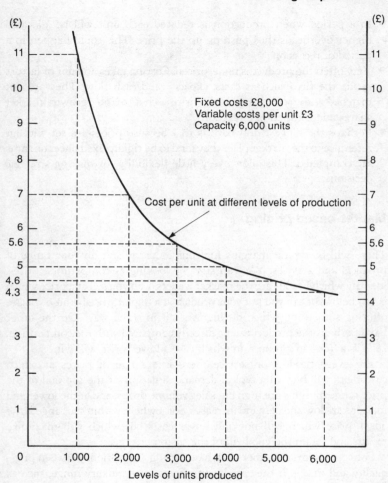

(£) ... (£)

Fixed costs £8,000
Variable costs per unit £3
Capacity 6,000 units

Cost per unit at different levels of production

Levels of units produced

**Fig. 7.1** Cost plus graph

approach to costing and pricing is widely practised, and because it involves meticulous fact gathering and calculations it is considered by many to be scientifically correct, this is especially so in manufacturing industries. However, there are a number of other flaws in this method of pricing:

● It is a common mistake to assume that you can sell enough units at cost plus price to give the required rate of return. Overheads are divided across the number of units produced, and if all the units are not sold within the trading period the amount of overheads recovered from sales will be insufficient to cover the bills.

- In a period when production is reduced each unit will be allocated higher overheads thus pushing up the price. This could happen in a period of recession.
- Very often the product is underpriced. Costing takes account of factors inside the firm such as costs, capacity and cash flow. They are not matched with factors outside the firm, such as market growth, market shares and competitors' reactions.
- Perhaps the biggest drawback is that because prices are set without reference to the market place they tend to be rigidly fixed once the sums are completed. This allows very little flexibility for making strategic decisions.

## Market-based pricing

There will be typical margins for your industry, and on your range of products and services. You can start by looking at competitors' prices. Identify which brands are the market leaders. Can you sell at a price which is just below, or can you put your product at a higher price because you are offering something which distinguishes it in some way? On the other hand perhaps the product can be directly compared with the competition, i.e. it is a 'me-too' product, in which case a lower price will win.

For every product or service there is a range of prices at which customers will buy. In a typical demand situation, at the top end of the price range margins are high but sales volume drops, and at the lower end margins are low and demand increases. Somewhere within the range is the 'ideal' price which will not only cover costs but which will maximize profits and retain the goodwill of the customer.

For some items customers will have strong associations between price, quality and image. If they are buying items in the luxury range, such as perfumes, designer clothes and furniture, works of art, etc., they expect to pay a high price in return for exclusive design, high quality workmanship, or a share in the Rolls Royce image.

One cosmetics company, having launched a large bottle of perfume in its spring catalogue, found that sales were not reaching targets. As a result the product was withdrawn for a season and then reintroduced in the following year. This time the product was halved in size and doubled in price. As a result sales increased dramatically, thus showing that in the perfume market customers equate 'expensive' with 'value' and 'exclusivity'.

When a product or service is notably different in an advantageous way, or if the product itself is unique, customers will be prepared to pay a high price. However, obvious high margins will attract competition, and the market will be sensitive both to competitor response and to different forms of the product. Nevertheless, if your product is one which can be changed and adjusted on an individual basis, you are probably in a position to charge what the market will bear, more especially if your customers do not have contact with one another.

Many small businesses underprice in the belief that a low price strategy will attract customers away from the competition. Low price means lower margins, unless output can be increased significantly, thereby reducing unit costs and increasing total sales. The small firm is rarely in a position to increase output greatly, consequently you can be working at full capacity only to find that you are not generating enough profits for replacement and growth. On the whole, low price strategy is the weakest approach to product differentiation.

Getting the price right is a difficult task. Successful companies will match prices to markets while weaker companies will base their prices on costs, and set them without regard to the market. Pricing should be determined after account has been taken of:

- Product differentials
- Customer attitudes
- Potential and existing competitor response
- Promotional activities
- Costs.

The product's position on the product life cycle will also affect your pricing policy.

- New products launched at high prices will attract competitors who may take away the market by launching similar products at lower prices.
- New products launched at lower prices may make it difficult for competitors to enter the market profitably.
- Price is not a primary consideration to the customer when a new product is at a high growth stage. This presents profit opportunities.
- If the product is at a mature position on the product life cycle then a reduction may help maintain market share, and continue to provide profit contribution.

Figure 7.2 illustrates the strategies employed by applying different combinations of price and product quality to the market.

Price

|  | High | Medium | Low |
|---|---|---|---|
| High | Premium | Market penetration | Super bargain |
| Medium | Overpricing | Average quality | Bargain |
| Low | Hit & run | Shoddy goods | Cheap goods |

Product quality

**Fig. 7.2** Different strategies using a combination of price and quality

## Are you making a profit?

Once you have decided on the right price for the market it is crucial to assess your margins and the effects they will have on overall profitability and cash requirements. It was seen earlier that using costs as a basis for pricing was less effective than market-based pricing. However, costs must be a consideration and should be used as a measure to test the viability of a price.

It is important that you capture information on all the costs of your business. These costs can be broken down into two categories: *fixed costs* and *variable costs*. Fixed costs are those which must be paid regardless of production and sales. Variable costs are those costs, such as materials, which increase with production.

Examples of fixed costs:

- Rent and rates
- Depreciation (an important element which is often forgotten)
- Promotion, selling and distribution costs
- Finance costs
- Heat and light
- Administration costs, salaries, etc.

Examples of variable costs:

- Raw materials
- Direct labour
- Power used for production

Some costs are difficult to allocate. For instance, electricity will have a fixed element for heating and lighting, and a variable element for the power used in production.

Let us now take the simple figures outlined in the cost-plus example. The organization has enough capacity to produce 6,000 units per month, and fixed costs are £8,000 per month. Each item has variable costs of £3 (materials, labour and power).

The company has assessed the competition and the market place, and feels that the best price the market will allow is £5. At this price can the business make a profit, and how long will it take to break even? A few simple calculations will provide the answer.

When one unit is sold how much does it make? By subtracting variable cost from selling price we find that it makes a contribution of £2. What exactly is contribution? It can hardly be called 'profit' when there are £8,000 of fixed costs still to pay off.

Once 4,000 units have contributed £2 each, a total of £8,000, then fixed costs are covered. This is the break-even point. At this point revenue flowing in from sales exactly equals the total costs flowing out.

The next unit, number 4,001, will make a contribution of £2. Since fixed costs are now covered, this £2 can be called 'profit'. Every unit after the break-even will make a £2 contribution to profit.

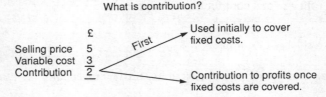

What is contribution?

| | £ | |
|---|---|---|
| Selling price | 5 | |
| Variable cost | 3 | |
| Contribution | 2 | |

First — Used initially to cover fixed costs.

Contribution to profits once fixed costs are covered.

If production stopped before the break-even the cash flowing out would be greater than the cash flowing in and the business would make a loss. Figure 7.3 illustrates this point.

It would be highly impractical to draw a graph every time you wanted to assess profits or break-even at different prices or at different production levels. Graphs are rarely so accurate that exact data can be taken from them, but they serve to provide an excellent visual presentation for facts and figures.

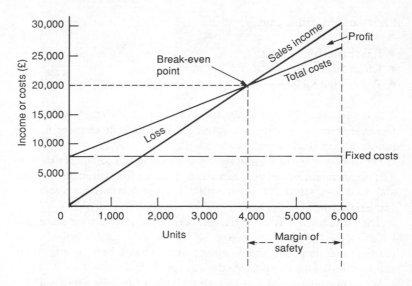

**Fig. 7.3** Break-even graph

We can quickly work out profits and break-even using the following simple formulae:

1. Contribution per unit = Selling price – Variable cost

2. Break-even = $\dfrac{\text{Total fixed costs}}{\text{Contribution per unit}}$ = No. of units

3. Profit = Total contribution – Fixed costs

In the case of our example:

Break-even = $\dfrac{£8,000}{£2}$ = 4,000 units (£20,000 revenue)

Profit     = (6,000 × £2) – £8,000 = £4,000

It should be possible to work out profits or losses at any level of production (e.g. at 3,500 units the loss would be £1,000). Better still, it is possible to test the effect of price changes. For example, a price increase of 25p on the above would reduce the break-even to 3,555 units, and raise profits to £5,500, a fairly significant profit increase (37%) for a small increase in price (5%).

Contribution is the key to assessing viability of price. Each of your products will provide a contribution. If this is expressed as a percentage of price – in the example it is a 40% margin – you can quickly calculate the gross margin you can expect at any forecast level of sales.

## Example

Forecast

| Product | No. of units | Contribution margin % | Total sales £ | Contribution £ |
|---------|--------------|-----------------------|---------------|----------------|
| A | 3,000 | 30 | 18,000 | 5,400 |
| B | 2,000 | 35 | 14,000 | 4,900 |
| C | 1,000 | 40 | 5,000 | 2,000 |
| | | | 37,000 | 12,300 |

$$\text{Gross margin on forecast sales} = \frac{£12,300}{£37,000} \times 100 = 33.24\%$$

In the above example a producer might wish to increase the overall margin by changing the product mix. There will be a number of areas for consideration; these will include asking the following questions.

- Is it possible to increase sales for any one of the products?
- Are there any limitations on skills or materials availability which might affect any proposed changes?
- Is there sufficient capacity?
- Is it necessary to maintain the present mix in order to satisfy customer needs? Should this be a priority?
- Does the present product mix, and resulting margins, meet the overall objectives of the company?

Contribution analysis can prove useful in making decisions about pricing, product range and type of market. It can also be used to great effect in assessing contribution from departments, a section of floor space, a geographical area, a type of outlet, etc., thus assisting your management team in planning exercises.

## The consequences of growth

Business expansion usually involves further investment. New premises, or extensions and alterations to the existing premises, and the purchase of capital items can cause a sudden rise in fixed costs. Higher levels of working capital will be needed for staffing, extra stocks and other increased activity.

Profits will be absorbed into all of these areas, and if further finance has to be obtained then the cost of borrowing will increase fixed costs still further.

Expansion may take place in incremental steps over a period of time, or in one large initial step, which could be brought about by moving premises, followed by gradual stages. The effect of a step in overheads is a sudden reduction in profits. We are expecting sales to increase, but the actual results will be in the form of an upward tilt in the sales curve, rather than a sudden jump to match costs. Consequently if expansion takes place during a profitable period the business is likely to find that the margin of safety (i.e. the period of time during which all contribution is profit) has been eroded.

Figure 7.4 illustrates how a step up in 'fixed costs' will affect 'total costs'. In this example the new total costs do not actually meet the sales line. But in some cases this might happen, which would then create a new break-even point. In other circumstances the total cost line might actually cross the sales line thus taking the business into a temporary loss-making situation.

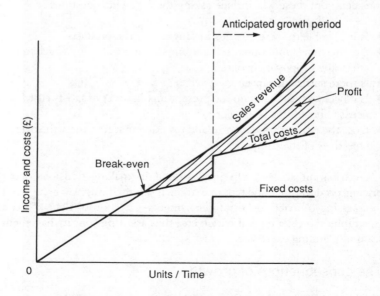

**Fig. 7.4** How profit is affected by a step up in costs

Figure 7.4 serves to point out the importance of time scales. If the bottom line of the graph were measured in time as well as units, it might be possible to schedule growth plans so that there is provision for some degree of margin of safety. The graph highlights the need for more knowledge and certainty of markets and suppliers. It also helps to emphasize the requirement for better controls when your firm is undertaking a growth programme.

## How does the buyer decide?

Price, although important, is rarely the only factor taken into account by the customer. Your product or service represents a bundle of factors which are ranked by the buyer according to his own specific needs. These could include:

- design and skills
- quality
- materials used
- after-sales service
- packaging and presentation
- compatibility
- price.

Your earlier market and product research will have highlighted the product differentials most valued, and you will now have a profile of the existing customer which outlines his style and tastes. Hopefully you are aware of further marketing opportunities available for satisfying the needs of your customers and those of potential customers.

At this point it would be useful to examine the position and behaviour of the buyer. We have established that individuals have a need for products which perform more than their basic functions. Take for example, hand-made Italian shoes – the customer is more likely to purchase them because they create an image, although there will be other expectations such as comfort, foot protection and price-value associations.

When the buyer has a need he or she goes through a preliminary process of seeking and contemplating the benefits. In the case of shoes the buyer may examine factors such as design, colour, durability, material and price. When offered a choice between products he or she is faced with the task of making a decision. The example below is based on buying a car, and illustrates just how complex the decision might be:

---

**The purchase decision for buying a car**

| | | No. of decisions |
|---|---|---|
| (a) | Choose to buy a particular car. | 1 |
| (b) | There are ten models. | 10 |
| (c) | There are two types of gearbox. | 2 |
| (d) | Choice of eight colours. | 8 |
| (e) | Gloss or metallic finish? | 2 |
| (f) | There are four interior trims. | 4 |
| (g) | Which of three dealers? | 3 |

In total there are:

$1 \times 10 \times 2 \times 8 \times 2 \times 4 \times 3 = 3,840$ routes for decision.

---

The complexity of the buying process depends on the buying situation, and is often related to the value of the purchase. Buying a packet of sugar is a simple process, buying a computer is very complex. The buyer will finally choose the product which is felt to provide the best satisfaction for his or her perceived needs, functional and otherwise.

Once the decision has been made the purchaser will now suffer a degree of post-purchase anxiety. This is directly related to the complexity of the decision and the amount paid. Could it be the wrong decision? Could it have been bought cheaper elsewhere? He or she will look for reassurance. The new car owner starts to look out for similar models on the roads, and will feel even more reassured when advertisements appear to leap from the pages of every magazine which extol the virtues of the chosen vehicle, or which compare it favourably with another make of car.

The supplier can reduce the anxiety by offering guarantees, warranties, service contracts and spare parts facilities. The car owner may now feel that he is part of a family or a club, especially if further information in the form of magazines and leaflets *follow* the purchase.

## Summary

Pricing policy is aimed at finding the 'right price', which will satisfy customers and at the same time provide an acceptable contribution to the business.

'Cost plus' pricing is a commonly used method of pricing. It is based on *Labour + Materials + A share of the overheads + Profit*. However, there are problems related to the way in which overheads are allocated which make this method unsatisfactory.

Market based pricing will include examining the prices of your competitors, and looking for the range of prices customers are prepared to pay for any product. Somewhere within the range is the ideal price which will serve to maximize profits.

Customers have strong associations with price. High price is equated with luxury or high quality, and there are certain 'psychological' prices which are acceptable. Product differentials will often induce customers to pay higher prices. In setting price you will need to consider the product's position on the product life cycle. Policy will differ for new products and those at a mature phase.

Break-even analysis is a useful method for assessing margins. Contribution analysis can be used for deciding on products and product mix.

Growth will cause a step-up in fixed costs. The effect will be greatly reduced profits, and sometimes the business will be placed in a temporary loss-making situation.

7

## Checklist

---

1. Can you identify similar products to yours in the market place? Do you know all the prices offered by the competition?
2. Do you follow market leaders when setting prices? Do you price below, above or the same?
3. Is your product sufficiently different from competing goods to allow for higher prices?
4. Are you in a position to charge what the market will bear?
5. Can you identify total fixed costs for one year?
6. Can you identify variable costs for each product?
7. Do you know the contribution for each product?
8. Do you know what product mix will give the best overall contribution? Can you achieve the required sales for each product?
9. Is there any limiting factor which will prevent you from producing the best product mix?
10. Do you know the break-even point for each product or service?

---

# 8 Controlling working capital

How much working capital? □ The cash flow forecast □ The problems of controlling working capital □ Summary □ Checklist

The balance sheet lists the current value of the assets of the business and tells you how they were funded. It is simply a snapshot of the situation at a given date. In the example given in Fig. 8.1 funding, provided by the shareholders and by retained profits, has been used to fund fixed assets and working capital.

| BALANCE SHEET | | |
|---|---|---|
| FIXED ASSETS | £ | £ |
| | | 190,000 |
| CURRENT ASSETS: | | |
| Stocks | 130,000 | |
| Debtors | 90,000 | |
| Bank | 8,000 | |
| | 228,000 | |
| LESS CURRENT LIABILITIES: | | |
| Creditors | (£115,000) | |
| WORKING CAPITAL (net current assets) | | 113,000 |
| NET ASSETS | | 303,000 |
| FINANCED BY: | | |
| Share capital | 200,000 | |
| Profit & loss account | 103,000 | 303,000 |

**Fig. 8.1**  Example of a balance sheet

## How much working capital?

Working capital is the amount of money available for financing all the running costs of the business, including purchase of stocks and raw materials. It is the money which will be used to generate profits and is therefore vital to the success of the business. In the balance sheet in Fig. 8.1 there is £8,000 in the bank, but this is only part of the working capital. The true working capital figure at the date of the balance sheet is £113,000. This is worked out by subtracting *current liabilities*, i.e. creditors, from *current assets*, i.e. stock + debtors + cash. The remainder of the funding is tied up in fixed assets of £90,000.

The diagram in Fig. 8.2 represents a small toy manufacturing company, and £113,000 has been invested in working capital. The arrows represent the cycle of the working capital through a period of time.

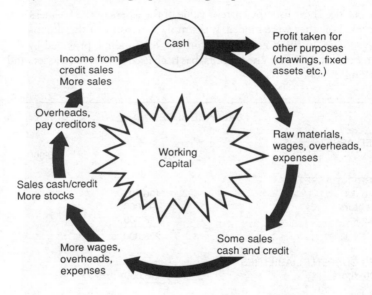

**Fig. 8.2** The working capital cycle

Once activity begins, money starts to flow out. Raw materials are purchased (some on credit), wages have to be paid weekly, and there are regular payments for general overheads and expenses. Sooner or later the raw materials are turned into stocks of finished goods, but before these are all sold, more raw materials must be purchased for the next round of manufacturing. There will be further labour and overhead payments, and on top of this, suppliers are starting to demand payment for the raw materials purchased earlier on credit.

So far the cash has been flowing out. However, some cash will eventually start to flow in from the customers (who wisely will have taken the maximum credit period allowed). Once the cycle is established the inflows and outflows will each develop their own regular patterns. However, there is one important difference, the money flowing in should be greater than the money flowing out, because it has profits attached to it. The profits are drawn off for other purposes, but the working capital should remain in the business at the same level.

The most important element in this money cycle is time. The more often you can turn over the working capital then the more efficiently it is working for you. The ratio of working capital to profits is greatly enhanced. For example, two identical companies earn profits of £10,000 each. One company has working capital of £5,000, and the other has £2,500. The working capital of the first company has a ratio of 2 : 1, the other has a ratio of 4 : 1, in other words the second firm is twice as efficient.

When a business undergoes a period of growth there is a need for increased levels of working capital for funding the increase in stock purchase and overheads. A great number of small firms run their businesses with insufficient funds and as a consequence they are always struggling to keep up with cash flow. On paper the profit and loss account is showing profits, but in reality there is no cash. Often profits have been drawn into the working capital cycle in order to reduce prohibitive overdraft levels. Consequently a growth opportunity can create very real cash flow problems. This reason alone causes many businesses to fail.

On the other hand many firms choose to borrow some or all of the working capital, and are also very successful and efficient. The difference lies in the preparation. They have borrowed enough, at a known rate of interest, and over a planned period of time. Their planning has taken interest charges and overdraft reduction into account, and they have thus known what minimum sales targets they must achieve.

In deciding on working capital needs the following points need to be considered:

(a) Anticipated activity levels – this will require forecasting sales and working from this to estimate all the costs involved, and the anticipated income.

(b) Expansion or growth plans for the future, and the time scales for each step. All the costs need to be worked out.

(c) Allowing for possible problems such as hold-ups and inefficiencies which may cause delay – keeping in mind that time is money.

(d) The cost of borrowing, and repayment periods.

Your firm will need an increased investment in working capital so that you can fund stocks, staff and other overheads. The key to knowing how much you need in working capital is to draft a cash flow forecast.

## The cash flow forecast

The cash flow forecast is a simple document in layout, but tedious and time-consuming to draw up. Consequently many owner/managers engage people outside the business to carry out this enormously important exercise in planning. Worse still, some put the finished document in a filing cabinet and forget about it until the next year.

The cash flow forecast is basically an expression of all your previous planning. You have all the facts and information relative to the plan's interpretation into figures, and therefore you will need to be influential in its design. It is *an essential planning document*.

The document can be laid out in a number of styles; all of the clearing banks are happy to supply their own forms to clients. A simpler approach is to use a computer spreadsheet which serves two purposes: first the computer does all the calculations, and secondly it is very easy to change and move items around so that you can test 'what if' situations.

## A measure of liquidity

A cash flow forecast looks at the future. However, it does *not* measure profit. The 'bottom line' of a cash flow is a measure of liquidity, i.e. cash available or not available at a particular time. Properly drawn up, it shows where cash is coming from, how it is spent and, more important, when these inflows and outflows will take place. It is designed to draw attention to the future need for an overdraft, loan or capital injection, and will thus assist in forward financial planning. More simply, the cash flow is the money cycle. 'Cash' means all sums deposited and drawn on the bank account.

Figure 8.3 shows a section of a simple cash flow situation. The firm is expanding, and new equipment recently purchased must be paid for in February. Sales of finished goods and purchases of raw materials are increasing. Suppliers give a month's credit but it takes one and a half months to make the goods and a further two months to sell and collect the cash. Orders are flowing in.

Here is the proof of the old saying 'time is money'. If it takes three and a half months for the progress of raw materials into cash, and suppliers want payment at the end of one month (overheads and labour want payment too), *the time lag creates a shortage of cash*. The cost of borrowing is directly related to that length of time. If we shorten the time span from three and a half months to, say, two months, the cost of borrowing is significantly reduced. Even if we are able to finance the time lag without borrowing, there is still a cost – this is the 'opportunity cost'

Cash flow forecast for six months

| | January £ | February £ | March £ | April £ | May £ | June £ |
|---|---|---|---|---|---|---|
| (Sold 2 months ago) | | | | | | |
| *Receipts* | | | | | | |
| Cash sales | 2,000 | 2,000 | 2,200 | 2,200 | 2,000 | 2,000 |
| Credit sales | 180,000 | 190,000 | 160,000 | 120,000 | 130,000 | 140,000 |
| Other receipts | 600 | – | – | – | – | – |
| Total A | 182,600 | 192,000 | 162,200 | 122,200 | 132,000 | 142,000 |
| *Payments* | | | | | | |
| Creditors – materials | 120,000 | 100,000 | 110,000 | 120,000 | 140,000 | 150,000 |
| Wages & salaries | 10,000 | 10,000 | 12,000 | 13,000 | 13,000 | 14,000 |
| Heat, light, power | – | – | 3,500 | – | – | 2,600 |
| Rates | – | – | – | 1,500 | – | – |
| Advertising | 2,500 | – | 1,500 | – | 1,500 | – |
| Other expenses | 3,400 | 3,000 | 4,000 | 4,100 | 800 | 900 |
| Loan | 1,500 | 1,000 | 1,500 | 1,500 | 1,500 | 1,500 |
| Tax | – | – | – | – | – | 5,000 |
| Capital items | – | 50,000 | – | – | – | – |
| (Purchased 1 month ago) Total B | 137,400 | 164,000 | 132,500 | 140,100 | 156,800 | 174,000 |
| Cash at start | (100,000) | (54,800) | (26,800) | 2,900 | (15,000) | (39,800) |
| Cash increase/decrease (A – B) | 45,200 | 28,000 | 29,700 | (17,900) | (24,800) | (32,000) |
| Cash at end | (54,800) | (26,800) | 2,900 | (15,000) | (39,800) | (71,800) |

**Fig. 8.3** Example of a cash flow forecast

of being able to use the money in other ways, e.g. to gain interest from a deposit account.

The 'top line' of the cash flow is the translation of your sales forecast into timings of receipts from customers. In fact the whole cash flow forecast is based upon the sales forecast, thus the degree of accuracy depends on how well you have undertaken your marketing research and designed your marketing plan.

The cash flow is both a planning tool and a management tool. Each month, or budget period, the actual inflows and outflows will be measured against the projected figures for that period and appropriate action taken if necessary.

## The problems of controlling working capital

Small firms are frequently undercapitalized. As previously stated many get into trouble because of cash flow, even when the order book is full. The following list outlines some of the causes.

## Overstocking

Every time you purchase stock you are putting some of your working capital on the shelf. The longer it stays there the longer it is unable to 'work', i.e. generate profits.

Obviously you will need to keep sufficient stock, and certainly for the retailer it is important to stock a shop so that it creates an 'illusion of choice' for the customer. You will also need to stock enough to cover suppliers' lead times, and a little more for emergency cover. However, kleptomania rules in some warehouses. There are those who feel they are not in business unless they can see boxes piled up to ceiling height, and shop-owners who believe that they must keep every item in a range, and in every size and colour.

## Giving lengthy credit

If debtors are taking too long to pay the result is that you are financing your customers' businesses by putting working capital on their shelves. At the same time the actual cost of the working capital is increasing and therefore your profit margin on the sale is being eroded. You lose on two counts: (a) the money is not available to work for you, and (b) the cost of borrowing.

Credit control is an aspect of your administration which needs to be carefully monitored. Disciplining customers to pay on time by setting credit periods, offering discount incentives, prompt invoicing, sending statements and chasing them is a priority. A good system will keep track of debtors and should regularly produce aged debtors lists, i.e. information on who owes, how much, for how long.

Another important aspect of credit control is the evaluation of your customers' creditworthiness. One large bad debt is often sufficient to cripple a small firm. Ask for trade references from other suppliers, and take up bank references. If potential customers are limited companies you can refer to the financial accounts of the business; however, these are not always up to date. Set ceilings on the amount of credit a customer can have, and regularly check that it is not being exceeded. Be extra careful of the levels of credit given to new customers, and be wary of the customer who suddenly places a very large order.

A small company will often be delighted to get an order from a very large company. Unfortunately one of the biggest problems is that many large companies are extremely slow payers. The author has had dealings with large firms who have taken up to six months to pay, and have helped themselves to discounts as well. The blame is almost always placed on their computer systems, and of course they realize that you are unlikely to take them to court for 2%, especially if you want more orders. How can you deal with this problem?

First of all decide whether or not your small firm can afford to finance a large company for that amount and for that period of time – in other words do you really need them? Most small firms are reluctant to part with their larger clients, partly because they feel that a large company is capable of greatly increasing their fortunes, and because they feel some sense of security in knowing that they will get paid eventually. On the other side, if all of your dealings are on a regular basis with large firms, then once the cash starts to flow in it will come in at regular intervals. You only need to finance the first time lag.

If you are going to trade with a large company then make sure you get the name of the person who is responsible for writing the cheques, so that you can bombard him with telephone calls and letters if necessary. Ensure that the prices you offer are sufficient to cover some of the costs, should you have to wait for payment.

Many owner/managers are fearful of upsetting customers by chasing them for payment, some even feel that it is 'ungentlemanly', and will result in a loss of business. However, most businesses have respect for companies who appear efficient in chasing outstanding debts, the assumption being that they are efficient in all aspects of the business.

8

## Pushing creditors too far

Trade credit is an excellent short-term means of financing a business. Creditors supply goods and allow payment within a fixed period of time. Often they add an incentive to pay by offering a cash discount. If you are in the happy position of being able to sell the goods before having to pay for them then the whole transaction has been financed by the supplier; such a situation might occur in the fresh food trade, or a flower shop. Overall, the credit period allows time to move production and marketing processes a stage forward.

'Leaning on the trade', i.e. helping yourself to longer credit periods than suppliers have offered, is a useful way of helping overcome cash flow problems. Unfortunately there are a few obvious and hidden costs attached to this.

(a) By stretching the credit period you will lose the cash discount. For large orders this may be significant. However, this is not always relevant if money has to be borrowed in order to pay the bill.

(b) The growing business needs to consider very carefully the goodwill of its suppliers. By building up a good reputation of prompt and early payments, the owner/manager of a small firm will have little difficulty in getting bigger credit limits when the need arises.

(c)  When your firm reaches a point where it is able to place substantial orders, your reputation for quick settlement will provide the edge for negotiating better trade and cash discounts, because you are now an extremely valued customer.

In general, the advice is to take cash discounts if cash flow allows, otherwise simply pay on time. In a situation where you are unable to pay on time talk to the suppliers.

## High living habits

Earlier it was stated that when working capital turns over in the business it generates profits which can be taken out for other purposes. Once all running costs have been covered profits can be used in a number of ways:

- For replacing or reducing the overdraft
- The reduction of long-term loans
- The purchase of capital items
- For taking by the owner as drawings.

Decisions on drawings and expenditure on capital items are made prior to the start of the financial year; these amounts are drawn off during the trading year. This means there is a need of advance planning of profits as well as cash levels. The younger the business the harder it is to forecast sales and plan profits. Consequently mistakes often occur, such as when owners decide on a personal life-style which the business cannot afford, i.e. they develop the 'BMW syndrome'.

If drawings are in excess of profits then working capital becomes depleted. Borrowing increases, until eventually you are running the business for the benefit of the lenders. If this is added to other forms of inefficient management – and it usually is – it becomes difficult to keep the lenders happy, and a whole vicious circle develops.

## Buying costly assets

This is similar to the previous example, and the two often go together. In this case working capital is removed from the working situation and turned into capital items (machines etc.).

The first rule is never to use the allocated working capital for buying fixed assets. The decision to buy fixed assets should be made at the planning stage, which is well in advance of the date of purchase. Separate provision should be made to cover the cost, this can be in the form of borrowing by fixed term loan, putting in more owner's capital, or planning to use profits. The second rule is to assess the cost of the asset against the needs of the business. Is it needed? Can we afford this model? Will a cheaper one do?

The message is, do not buy unnecessary or extravagant items which may not be used to sufficient capacity, or for which a more serviceable version will perform the same tasks with the same efficiency, *at a time when the budget is stretched.*

## Overstaffing

Staff time represents outflow of funds. Each hour uses up a fraction of working capital. We have noted that idle stock is cash sitting on the shelves with some costs attached; however, idle man-hours represent an actual loss of cash, i.e. it depletes the working capital significantly.

For example, in one organization four people were engaged in food preparation. They worked in a small area using specialist equipment. It was also noted that only two people at a time could work because of lack of space, so they took it in turns. In effect the labour content had doubled, but this was not costed into the product, and as a result it was not recouped in sales.

Costs can be controlled by keeping staff levels to a sensible minimum, so that each person has a reasonable workload, and by providing the right working conditions so that they can perform their tasks efficiently. Part-time staff normally provide good value in some areas of the firm. Someone who is employed for four hours in a day is likely to have less 'down time' pro rata than a person who works a seven hour day.

## Overtrading

Getting bigger usually involves an increase in sales activities. The order book is looking healthy and the organization engages in expanding premises, machines, staff, etc.

One problem often associated with businesses which expand too rapidly is that of overtrading. In this case more orders have been accepted than the company's resources can cope with. Extra stocks are purchased, staff are overstretched and cannot meet time scales, extra staff are taken on, overtime rates are paid, and lack of space and machinery creates immediate problems.

Frequently customers are let down, and if they in turn are working to tight schedules the goodwill factor is seriously damaged. Cash flow becomes a problem because no provision has been made for extra working capital, and therefore it is difficult to pay suppliers and staff. Suppliers threaten to cut off supply of materials before work is completed, and the relationship is soured. Banks and other investors tend to be unsympathetic too, because this type of crisis management usually recurs in the same firms time and again.

What should a company do if a large number of orders come in at once? It is very difficult to turn away a lucrative deal, and there is always the possibility of losing that customer. However, you have to balance the loss of an order against the loss of a company. Diplomatic handling is important in order to keep customer goodwill. It might be feasible to offer a future date, or even to arrange a subcontract with a competitor.

---

1. Using your end of year balance sheets for the past three years, work out the levels of working capital. Measure for each year:

   (i)  Working capital as a ratio to turnover.
   (ii) Working capital as a ratio to gross profits.

   If the ratio is low for any period is this because:

   (a) *Stock levels were too high.* Can this be attributed to inefficiency, or to a special purchase for a large order?
   (b) *Cash at bank was too high*, therefore finances were liquid but not working?
   (c) *Debtors figure was unusually high.* Is this due to a sudden increase in sales at the end of the year or is this due to poor credit control?

2. Work out the average length of credit offered to customers for each of the three years by the following method:

$$\frac{\text{Debtors}}{\text{Sales}} \times 365 = \text{Number of days}$$

   Has your collection period improved?

3. Examine your credit control system.

   (a) When are the invoices dispatched? Is it immediately or at the end of the month?
   (b) Are monthly statements sent out?
   (c) Is there an aged debtors list? Who controls it?
   (d) What is the procedure for chasing debtors?
   (e) What is the level of bad debts?

4. How many employees have you got? Estimate:

   (a) Sales per employee.
   (b) Gross profit per employee.
   (c) Any expense per employee.

   e.g. $\dfrac{\text{Sales}}{\text{No. of employees}}$ = Sales per employee

   Compare the three years.

---

## Summary

Working capital is shown on the balance sheet as: Current assets *less* Current liabilities. It is the money which generates profits. It flows out to buy labour, overheads and stock, and eventually flows in as payments from debtors. This receipt has profit attached to it.

The most important element of the money cycle is time, since the more often you can turn over the working capital the more profits will be generated. A growing business will need increased levels of working capital for financing higher stock levels, increased overheads and a higher level of sales.

The cash flow forecast helps to plan the inflows and outflows of cash, and is an essential planning document for helping maintain and monitor liquidity.

Controlling working capital means ensuring that: the stock levels are kept to suitable levels; there is sufficient credit control; owners do not spend the working capital on costly capital items; and that the organization is not overstaffed or running inefficiently.

8

## Checklist

---

1. Have you drawn up a cash flow forecast? Is this a once a year procedure?
2. Do you compare actual and budgeted figures?
3. How realistic is the sales forecast used for the top line?
4. Is the cash flow optimistic, pessimistic or realistic?
5. Have you allowed for seasonal fluctuations?
6. Have you filled in the receipts and payments *when* they occur, or have you divided figures evenly by 12?
7. Have you allowed for possible holdups and problems?
8. Do you have a credit control system?
9. Do you have a monthly aged debtors list?
10. Do you take action over slow payers, e.g. take them to court?
11. Do you send invoices out promptly? With the goods?
12. Are your stock levels too high? Could you reduce them?
13. Can you sell off obsolete and out of date items?
14. Do you have the right staff levels?
15. Do you take too much money out of the business for personal use?
16. Are the business assets too grand, or are there assets surplus to its needs?

---

# 9　Financing growth

The right financial mix □ Gearing up for expansion □ Finding the finance □ Can you improve your firm's cash flow? □ Can you get further assistance from the bank? □ 'Off the balance sheet' finance □ Sale and lease back □ Equity finance □ Can you get financial assistance from the public sector? □ Presenting your case for finance □ Summary □ Appendix

Classically, small businesses have started with personal funds or loans from members of the family, and possibly a bank overdraft or loan borrowed against personal security. Successful growth brings with it the need for additional funding. Profits will be ploughed back into assets and stock, but if your planning is geared towards any significant expansion, which may include buying major capital items and recruiting extra staff, then your resources may be overstretched, and growth will have to be financed to some extent by new funds injected into the business.

## The right financial mix

So far we have looked at ways of evaluating the business risk by assessing the opportunities for the products and services you are providing, and we have established the need for planning and forecasting. The other ingredient required is financial planning. One important aspect of your forward plan is identifying the right mix of funds needed, the actual amount required, and the time scales involved. Following this is the decision on the methods to be used in seeking funds at interest rates which are not too onerous.

Sound growth plans depend on a proper financial mix, matching the type of finance to the purpose for which it is to be used. Short-term finance is needed for working capital, i.e. it finances stock, work-in-progress, debtors. Medium-term finance, say one to six years, is needed for the purchase of machines and vehicles; and long-term finance is used for buildings, heavy plant and machinery, and land.

The right financial mix

| Type | Use | Source |
|------|-----|--------|
| Short-term finance | Stock, W-I-P<br>Debtors<br>Running costs | Bank overdraft<br>Partly from long-term<br>sources<br>Trade creditors |
| Medium-term finance<br>1–6 years | Vehicles<br>Machinery<br>Fixtures & fittings | Medium term loans<br>Hire purchase<br>Leasing |
| Long-term<br>finance – more<br>than 5/10 years | Goodwill<br>Land<br>Buildings<br>Heavy plant &<br>machinery | Share capital<br>Retained profits<br>Mortgages<br>Long-term loans |

## Gearing up for expansion

Your business should have a desirable equity base, i.e. sufficient owner's funding. In a small company borrowings usually range between 50 and 100 per cent of the owner's equity. A healthy balance sheet might show a 'gearing ratio' of 1:2 (or 50 per cent), i.e. one pound borrowed for every two pounds of equity. However, when a business is growing it can build up a considerable burden of debt which may ultimately equal or outweigh the owner's equity. The highly geared firm, where loans are far in excess of owner's equity, will need to generate greater gross margins than a low geared business in order to cover interest on borrowings, and at the same time sustain the relationship of net profit to capital employed (capital employed is owner's equity plus borrowings and is explored later in this chapter). Firms having to provide for huge loan repayments run a very high risk of insolvency. One business owner was so successful in expanding her business that after three years hard labour she suddenly realized that she was actually working for the bank!

Banks may impose a gearing limit of 1:1 so that there is a reasonable buffer of equity for absorbing any losses that may arise. In addition, business owners who have put less finance into the business than the lenders stand to gain from its success, but will lose little if the business fails. This creates a 'moral hazard' in that the business owner may be tempted to take excessive commercial risks which will affect the bank, and also the business's employees, suppliers and customers.

Banks follow a rule of thumb approach that gearing should not exceed 1:1, however, there are always exceptions where they will accept higher gearing where turnover is rapid and stocks are easily realizable. For a business which is efficiently run, and where prospects are good, the gearing ratio is less crucial. A high return on capital employed will mean that interest charges, etc., can be covered and still leave a healthy amount in the business. For a limited company, a useful measure is that net profit before interest and tax should cover interest charges at least twice. For the sole trader or partnership, deduct a sensible amount for drawings from the net profit before measuring against interest.

## Finding the finance

At this point it is worth reminding you that your bank manager and your accountant ought to be closely involved in helping you plan the best sources, the amount required and the tax implications. If you have consulted your advisers regularly, i.e. kept them on your team, they will have a good understanding of your business and should respond with the best advice. Consulting your bank manager does not necessarily mean you must use the bank as your source of finance. Note, too, that this is not a responsibility which should be delegated to your advisers.

Planning finance for growth is best undertaken well in advance. At the time you set your growth objectives and start to develop a detailed marketing plan, you will progress to planning, costing and budgeting for each activity. Your plans will include a cash flow forecast, a projected profit and loss account and a balance sheet. Profit projections have no measure of certainty, therefore you ought to prepare borrowing facilities in excess of the predicted need so that, if necessary, there is a cushion available.

Broadly, your finance for growth is likely to come from:

- Your firm's cash flow.
- Your bank.
- 'Off-balance sheet' finance, such as leasing and hire purchase.
- Additional capital that you, or others, introduce to the business.
- The public sector.

## Can you improve your firm's cash flow?

Before looking externally for finance you should work out the extent to which your growth could be financed by improved cash flow. The principal areas of your business requiring scrutiny are your stock levels and ordering procedures, credit control, payments to suppliers, calling-in of cash investments, cost-cutting in general and disposing of unwanted assets and obsolete stocks. You can eliminate non-essential outgoings which you have maintained for old times' sake rather than for what they contribute to the business (e.g. subscribing to an association that has outlived its usefulness).

Often the biggest single problem is that of slow payers, especially your large firm customers. Can you renegotiate with them? They now know you and might be more sympathetic than when you first contracted with them. Depending on your business you may make greater use of customer-financing where cash for the total final sum (or a percentage of it) is paid with the order. With long contracts, stage payments are desirable.

## Factoring and invoice discounting

If slow payers are a problem then factoring or invoice discounting are means of keeping the cash flowing inwards. The major banks have specialist subsidiaries which are among the institutions providing this type of service. With factoring you sell your claims on debtors to the factoring company. The debtors then normally deal direct with the factor, thus reducing your administrative burden. The factoring company pays the firm on an agreed schedule and, under many schemes, carries the risk of bad debts. The factor will require a service fee in the range of 0.5 to 2.5 per cent of turnover. In addition you will incur, for payments on account, a charge slightly above the cost of your overdraft.

With invoice discounting you turn your debtors' obligations into cash at less than face value. The debtors know nothing of the arrangement because you still collect the money and, usually, carry the risk of bad debts. This may appeal to you if you are satisfied with the administration of your sales ledger and wish to maintain your normal relationship with customers while improving your cash flow. You may be able to cover the whole of your sales ledger or a selection from it based on your larger clients. The cost of the service is expressed as a discount on the finance used and is calculated for each day's use. The interest rates are comparable with hire purchase charges.

Factoring and invoice discounting schemes both normally allow you to withdraw up to 80 per cent of total approved invoice value immediately. When assessing the cost/benefit equation of factoring you will have to take account of the direct savings in management time, fewer bad debts, and either the greater availability of funds or a reduction in the costs of financing debtors by alternative means. Your turnover must exceed £200,000 per year before factoring companies are interested in you.

Invoice discounting is normally available only to established firms. Responsibility for debt collection remains with the firm. Subject to these requirements the avenues are there for you to explore. Some schemes extend to export services with multi-currency accounting.

The government also helps exporters through the Export Credit Guarantee Department. The ECGD insures businesses against the risk of bad debts and helps them by giving guarantees to banks under which finance can be obtained, often at a favourable rate of interest.

Any improvement in cash flow will reduce the need to raise additional short-term finance.

## Can you get further assistance from the bank?

### Overdraft facility

Your first port of call for additional finance should be the bank. The bank's advice in helping you to match financial obligations to your planned expansion will be important. You will have established, or be in the process of establishing, your need for fixed interest capital. In considering your request for funds the bank will be influenced by a mixture of:

- the commercial viability of the proposal,
- the quality of your management,
- your financial soundness, and
- the availability of security.

9

You should not be seeking to finance long-term plans on an overdraft (or any other short-term facility). Given its flexibility and cheapness the overdraft is the most commonly used source of outside finance in small businesses. A carefully prepared business plan, which identifies working capital requirements, will help you secure any additional overdraft you may require. Once this has been obtained it must be controlled within the limit allowed. If it transpires subsequently that the limit of the overdraft is insufficient, then approach the bank and keep them fully informed. Businesses are ill-advised to stretch this facility by purchasing the odd fixed asset – overdrafts should be self-liquidating.

If you have previously demonstrated to the bank that your business can be relied upon to control the overdraft then your prospects will be enhanced. If the purpose is specific, such as the purchase of a short-lived asset (e.g. a vehicle) then the bank's short loan facility with its formalized repayment system will be appropriate.

### Term loans

Given the limitations of overdraft finance, banks offer other types of loans that are more appropriate for financing expenditure of a capital nature. Term loans repayable over periods ranging from 1 to 20 years provide a significant outlet for bank funds. Such loans, which can be tailored to your own circumstances, are very suitable for the purchase of fixed assets where the repayments are scheduled to match the stream of revenues that the assets will generate.

In time-scale terms this type of finance is either short-, medium- or long-term. These loans will normally be secured and the rates of interest may be fixed or variable. Even when there is an increase in a variable rate of interest the actual monthly repayments may remain unchanged as banks are prepared to lengthen the term of the loan to accommodate the higher charges. The converse is also true when the rate falls. Not surprisingly these schemes are popular among small firms.

Banks actively promote some interesting and novel term lending schemes for the small firms sector. At one end of the spectrum a small business can borrow up to £15,000 on a fixed rate basis for up to 10 years. The National Westminister's Business Development Loan gives up to 20 years' credit at a fixed rate of interest, which is higher when the loan is unsecured. Where the loan exceeds £15,000, a two year capital repayment holiday can be negotiated. The upper limit under this scheme is £250,000 but there are schemes which have no upper limit and/or incorporate a drawdown facility.

## Capital Loan Scheme

The National Westminister's equity finance package is marketed under the name Capital Loan Scheme and operated through a wholly owned subsidiary, NatWest Growth Options Ltd. The intention is to provide venture capital when conventional bank finance is not available. Finance is in the form of loans, for up to 10 years, of between £25,000 to £200,000, with NWGO taking an option to subscribe for part of the company's equity. The option, which can be exercised at any time during the repayment period, is for a minority shareholding, usually less than 25 per cent. This leaves control unaffected (the bank does not normally exercise its right to appoint a director) but gives the bank the opportunity of sharing in the future success of the venture.

The loans rank behind claims of other creditors except loans by the directors or shareholders. Consequently the money is virtually a part of the company's primary equity. The only security required is an unsupported guarantee of 25 per cent of the difference between the capital loan and their own financial contribution. This should ensure the continuing commitment of key directors.

Given that the early years of expansion may be difficult, repayment holidays for both principal and interest are available from the outset. The interest is charged at a fixed rate for the whole period of the loan.

Unless you are in the field of new, high risk research and development projects (hi-tech ventures can be accommodated) you are likely to be eligible and should consider this type of finance if normal bank loans are not possible. The facility is available for the purchase of new assets or general development of the company. The case of Hibass Photomec, from the *Nat West Small Business Digest* column 'How it works in practice', is given as an example in the appendix to this chapter.

## The Loan Guarantee Scheme

Another lending scheme which is 'special' is the Loan Guarantee Scheme which was introduced in 1981 with the specific aim of providing finance for small businesses. The scheme aims to encourage banks to lend to small businesses whose propositions are realistic but who would be unable to attract funds because of lack of track record, insufficient security, or for riskier ventures on which banks will not give loans.

The government guarantees repayment to the bank of 70 per cent of loans up to £100,000, given over two to seven years by the participating institutions, who take 30 per cent of the risk. If you borrow under this scheme you will be expected to pledge all of the business assets as security but the banker is unable to call upon you for personal security. Almost all businesses qualify and you will have to be in farming, banking, education, forestry, insurance, recreation or culture, tied public houses, or the estate or travel agency businesses before you are excluded.

You have to apply to the lending institution supplying the customary information. Provided the lender indicates that your plans are viable and that funding is approved under the scheme, the DOTI is unlikely to change the decision.

The Loan Guarantee Scheme could form a part of your normal borrowing package. You could combine a normal term loan, an overdraft facility and a loan under the scheme. You may have to pay 1.5 per cent more than normal commercial rates of interest and, in addition, you have to pay a premium of 2.5 per cent on the guaranteed proportion of the loan. The institutions participating in the scheme are listed at the end of this chapter.

## Other bank services

Banks are suppliers, through their subsidiaries, of instalment credit (i.e. industrial hire purchase) and leasing. (See 'off the balance sheet' finance below).

If your expansion is based on exporting for the first time then you can ask your bank to arrange to draw upon documentary credits established by the importer's bank. Also the bank can provide direct finance by advances or by discounting the bills that you draw on shipments.

## 'Off the balance sheet' finance

### Leasing

If you lease a lorry you will acquire use of the vehicle, but ownership remains with the finance house. This means it appears on their balance sheet but not your own, i.e. it is 'off your balance sheet'. Strictly speaking, leasing is not a method of financing but it is a means whereby you can reduce your need for capital. Sensibly used leasing can increase your options and may enable you to bring forward profitable schemes that would otherwise have to wait.

Leasing is most attractive when you can use scarce cash profitably in the mainstream business rather than on peripherals like fork-lift trucks and vehicles. Also, if you are faced with gearing limits on your medium-term borrowing, leasing might be the solution. You will also have the advantage of knowing from the outset where you are in terms of known payments for a known period.

Leases can run for up to 10 or 15 years but are generally much shorter. Often at the end of the lease, you will be able to retain the asset at a greatly reduced rent. You will need to check exactly what is on offer from the banks, who offer extensive leasing arrangements, and others who also arrange leasing. With a 'finance' lease you will probably be responsible for maintenance and insurance. If you have an 'operating lease' on equipment, such as photocopiers, you are purchasing not only the use of the equipment but also the care and maintenance. This will be useful if heavy maintenance costs are likely to arise in regard to equipment with which you are unfamiliar.

### Hire purchase

Hire purchase and other credit instalments operate for businesses in much the same way as in the retail trade. It can be set up quickly without legal fees. The payment instalments can be matched to the income flow generated from having the use of the asset which is the subject of the agreement.

The purchase of a capital item by hire purchase or bank loan will favourably affect your taxation position. The cost of the asset, whether or not it is paid for by the end of the financial year, will attract the normal capital allowances. In addition, the HP or bank interest paid in any tax period is charged against profits. An extra advantage is that all the VAT can be reclaimed at the end of the first quarter following purchase, thus helping cash flow. However, hire purchase often has one significant drawback, the rate of interest charged by the finance company over the period of the purchase. Frequently, the total cost of the asset can be more than doubled, therefore it is important to examine and compare the APR (Annual Percentage Rate) offered by different finance companies, and to work out the total cost of the asset. A bank loan is likely to be cheaper, but may not be an option if the company gearing is too high.

By contrast, total lease payments can be charged against profits and VAT can be reclaimed, but there are no capital allowances. The asset does not belong to the company, and the cost of leasing is high (which adds significantly to fixed overheads).

As you seek to acquire new equipment you will have to consider, preferably with the advice of your accountant, which of these alternative methods of outside finance is best for you.

## Sale and lease back

One potential source of long-term capital that we have not yet considered is sale and lease back of your business premises. If you own them you could possibly sell them to an institution like an insurance company or pension fund who would grant you a long lease. In this way you get capital and the use of the premises. Transactions of this type have to be carefully investigated as they are not advantageous to all firms, partly because of the taxation situation and other borrowing arrangements. Professional advice here is an absolute must.

## Equity finance

Can you raise additional capital from your own funds or from outside sources?

Small firms are often limited in their ability to plough adequate profits back into the business to finance growth, especially when the plans are of a more ambitious nature. In the existence and survival stages of business owner-managers have often been able to rely on their own funds, those from family and friends, and the bank. The 'success' or 'growth' stage for many small firm owners may mean broadening the base from which capital, particularly equity, is subscribed.

Owner-managers are often cautious, unduly so, about seeking equity from outsiders as it means a dilution in their stake in the business. However, your business will grow more rapidly when you are less dependent on your own resources, and that may be your overriding objective. Seeking equity from outsiders may be a matter of necessity if further loan capital would push your gearing to an unacceptably high level.

In any event there are a large number of organizations prepared to take a minority shareholding in a small business. Moreover, the advent of the Share Buy Back Scheme (Companies Act 1981) has increased the prospect of the investor taking his or her money back out of the business at a later date, while giving you the chance to regain a greater share of the equity. If you are not already a company your first step will be to incorporate (see Chapter 11).

## Selling shares to outsiders

By selling shares to outsiders you broaden the capital base without the immediate financial impositions that arise from loans. This, as noted, is at the expense of a dilution of your stake. However, you can retain control. You may also benefit by establishing a market value for your company, making it easier to attract funds later and even creating an exit route in the longer term.

Advice on the 'equity' package is important. The shares in the package may be ordinary, deferred, or redeemable. Preference shares may also be issued but they are more akin to loan capital as they have priority over ordinary shares in respect of dividends and repayment of capital in the event of liquidation. On the other hand, preference shares do not normally attract voting rights.

Who will supply you with equity finance? In other words, who will buy your shares?

1. Banks. As shown above (National Westminster Capital Loan Scheme) the banks, who traditionally never provided equity finance, are now involved. Originally this involvement was almost exclusively through their merchant bank subsidiaries but the 'special schemes' for small businesses provide a means of more direct involvement. Most clearing banks have created subsidiaries for the purpose. The banks seek no more than a minority holding and have the ability to combine equity with loan finance to meet individual needs.

2. Private sources and BES funds. You may have friends or acquaintances willing to invest, but this may not be spreading your net wide enough. Your solicitor, accountant or stockbroker might enable you to make the right contacts. Merchant banks can also help make the 'match' between you and potential investors. Private investors may be attracted if well-placed to benefit from the tax incentives provided under the Business Expansion Scheme (see below). If you are the specialist supplier of a

component to a large firm (who depends on you) they may wish to support your growth: it will be for you and your advisers to decide whether it would be prudent to give them a stake in your firm.

The Business Expansion Scheme was introduced by the government to encourage investment in the equity capital of unquoted companies. The minimum investment in any single company is £500 and the investor must leave his or her capital in the company for at least five years. The attraction to the investor is that he or she can claim tax relief on the investment. The maximum annual amount that will attract tax relief is £40,000, so an investor paying tax at the top rate of 40 per cent will secure an investment of £40,000 at a net cost of £24,000. When, in 1987/88, the top rate was 60 per cent, the same investment would have cost £16,000. Clearly, the lower the rate of tax the less promising the scheme becomes as a means of attracting equity finance. Nonetheless the incentive remains and, in addition, there is an exemption from capital gains tax for BES shares issued after 18 March 1986 on their first disposal (this may make it easier to buy back the shares). The scheme gives you the opportunity to use the money subscribed interest free for five years or longer. From your standpoint there are certain eligibility requirements. You must carry on a 'qualifying trade' which covers virtually the complete range of manufacturing, construction, tourism, wholesale, retail and other service industries. The main exclusions are companies in banking, leasing and hiring, share dealing, farming, and legal and accountancy services.

9

You may be able to organize your own issue of shares (with your professional advisers) but some individuals invest through specialist BES funds which pool investors' money to invest in a portfolio of companies. The fund may require representation on your board.

The advantages to you of the Business Expansion Scheme as an investee company are:

- The subsidy in the form of a tax relief to the investor may enable you to bid up the price of your shares.
- BES investors, as high rate tax payers, often seek capital gains rather than income and do not look for an immediate return.
- BES investors often look for exit after five years and this enables you to reappraise your position.
- BES funds can introduce management expertise.
- BES enables small firms to tap into funds that otherwise might not have been available.

There are costs involved and these should be carefully considered with the assistance of professional advice.

3. Institutional investors. In addition to BES funds there are others in this category. These include merchant banks, insurance companies,

pensions funds, venture capital funds and other specialist institutions. Certainly some of these sources would not have been open to you at the start-up stage and may not be available even now as they have minimum and maximum amounts in terms of funds injected. You should consider these sources as you may find some combination of the following benefits results:

- Institutional investors, unlike some private investors who see themselves as committing a high proportion of their wealth, rarely seek a close involvement in the firm. They may expect a non-executive place on the board and this may bring to it valuable advice and experience. They may seek an undertaking from you as to how the firm is to be run and call upon you to supply regular reports and accounts. Venture capital funds are different because they will require a 'hands-on' approach. These institutions have strict investment criteria and look for high risk/high return opportunities.
- They normally seek no more than a minority equity stake.
- They may provide assistance in the shape of packages, which include loans and redeemable shares, preference or ordinary.
- Some institutions specialize in particular industries (e.g. hi-tech-related enterprise) or situations (e.g. companies in Devon and Cornwall, or research and development). It is a help if someone understands your industry or situation and can offer advice as well as finance.

You would do well to consult the financial press (e.g. *Investors Chronicle* or *The Financial Times*) which from time to time publishes guides to the sources of development funds and venture capital facilities. Such guides indicate the maximum/minimum sums injected, the extent of the equity stake (e.g. 20 per cent), whether a seat on the board is required, type of industry or situation, and exit criteria. Some useful addresses that will help you track down institutional investors feature in the Appendix. A service that might be useful to you is that provided by Venture Capital Report Ltd, of Boston Road, Henley-on-Thames, RG9 1DY. Their monthly journal, which is distributed to subscribers wishing to make venture capital investments, contains details of selected companies and projects seeking finance. Also helpful is *The Venture Capital Report Guide to Venture Capital in the UK*, 4th edition, £35.00, available from the above address or Pitman Publishing.

One of the best institutions for your needs could be Investors in Industry (3i), in which the major banks are the majority shareholders. It channels different sorts of finance, including equity, to small firms and has done much to finance small firm expansion having invested in well over 9,000 companies, covering all industrial sectors, by the end of 1988.

## Can you make your shares more marketable?

Unlisted Securities Market (USM). It is unlikely that you will be at the stage of a Stock Exchange listing, for which you must have an aggregate value of shares at the commencement of dealing of £500,000. However, if you have reached the point of needing the advantages of a secondary market to make your new equity more marketable you could consider the Unlisted Securities Market for which there is no minimum size but you must be registered as a public company. There is also a small market (the Over-the-Counter Market) for small and medium-sized companies not qualified for the USM.

## Can you get financial assistance from the public sector?

There is a wide range of government incentives, some of which are available generally while others are targeted specifically at the small firms sector. Assistance is also available from local authorities. It is not possible here to give a full account of these numerous measures but you will find that leading accountants such as Peat Marwick and Hacker Young publish very useful guides, sometimes available free of charge. There is also the publication *Official Sources of Finance and Assistance for Industry* published by the National Westminister Bank at £18.00 and available from Pitman Publishing or the Business Information Section, Market Intelligence Department of the National Westminster Bank at 6th Floor, National House, 14 Moorgate, London EC2R 6BS. The book should, however, be used in consultation with an adviser or accountant. Some measures can be highlighted within this book as follows:

9

- Assistance is available in some regions in the form of preferential loans and grants for the purchase of property but applications for Regional Development Grants ended on 31 March 1988. Often the objective is to encourage firms to relocate in certain designated areas. You have to consider these options by comparing the boost to your finances with the costs of the exercise, including access to markets, supplies and labour and the effect on transport costs. British Coal Enterprise Ltd provides preferential loans for small firms wishing to purchase premises in coalfield areas.
- The Rural Development Commission, in co-operation with banks, provides loans in certain rural areas of England. There are agencies providing similar support in Wales and Scotland.
- English Estates (EE) provides workshops, factories, warehouses, offices, units for high-technology companies and craft homes on flexible sale or lease terms. EE offers a full professional design and build

service to cater for specialized property needs. It can also arrange mortgages with the major banks at favourable terms.

- Some Government measures are aimed at supporting projects in particular areas, viz: micro-electronics; robotics; fibre optics; computer-aided design, manufacture and production management; and flexible manufacturing systems. If these are in your sphere you can obtain details from the Small Firms Service or your local Enterprise Agency.

- If your expansion plans are based on a genuinely innovatory product or process you could apply to the National Research Development Corporation (NRDC) which will share your development costs in return for a percentage levy on sales. NRDC is an arm of the British Technology Group (BTG). A main aim of BTG is to license inventions developed by government research departments to private industry.

- The Government plays an important part in the medium-term fixed interest finance provided by the European Investment Bank for businesses which promote the interests of the community or regional development, or which are in areas of structural problems (e.g. high unemployment). Loans are for up to 50 per cent of the cost of capital expenditure with a fixed rate of interest over eight years. The government guarantees to protect borrowers against losses arising from adverse changes in exchange rates. These loans are cheaper than comparable loans from UK sources and they range from between £15,000 and £250,000. The European Coal and Steel Community can also provide subsidized loans if your expansion creates jobs in areas where there are coal or steel closures. The appendix sets out the agencies through which application for EIB or ECSC loans can be made.

Changes are constantly taking place as to the range and form of these support measures but now that you have been introduced to some of them you may, in your own interests, wish to enquire of such agencies as the Small Firms Service and/or obtain one of the publications which sets out to cover government assistance more fully.

## Presenting your case for finance

No matter which institutions or individuals back your proposed expansion they will need to be persuaded that the venture will be profitable and that the risks are controllable. Profitability is important because it paves the way for you to repay borrowed funds and the interest. Those who provide equity will be looking for capital growth and a dividend, although the former may be more important to some investors.

The method by which you approach your sources for finance depends on the type, amount and structure of finance sought. Lenders of short-term secured loans are generally less demanding than lenders of long-term unsecured loans, or those providing equity finance. In deciding how to present your case try putting yourself in the position of the money provider.

---

You will need a detailed plan that enables the lender to assess the viability of your proposal. Most financial organizations are likely to want information in the following areas:

- Your specific reasons for seeking finance. Is it to enable you to expand your trading base? Launch new products? Reduce your dependence on short-term finance?
- The amount of finance sought and the form in which it is requested. Time-scales are important, too, and details of security available.
- Details of existing borrowing and indebtedness.
- A history of the business. The current products and services and proposed changes should be disclosed. Details of numbers employed in each area of activity and the profitability thereof.
- Details of directors and others in the management team so that their experience, qualifications, and ages are shown. Also give the names of your professional advisers, e.g. accountant, solicitor, and bank. Many financiers back the management team rather than the ideas. It is their best safeguard against the risks of the venture.
- A description of the buildings and details of whether the tenure is freehold or leasehold.
- A description of the plant and equipment (whether it is owned or leased) and details of its age and condition.
- A description of how the firm is run. Your proposed backers will be interested in knowing what accounting, management information, and budgetary control systems you have in place. (These important issues are discussed in the next chapter.)
- An outline of the main risks of your venture and how you have thought through those risks.
- Detailed accounts covering the past three years, plus your projections for the future, covering up to three years. Make details of your calculations available.

**9**

---

Finally, allow adequate time for your backers to study your proposal. You and your advisers must in turn scrutinize any proposals made to you. Check that you have the right financial mixture and that you can comply with any conditions imposed, e.g. the prohibition on the creation of further charges on the assets of the business.

## Summary

Assess your financial needs. Do not embark upon growth under-financed. Sound growth depends on the right financial mixture. Match the type of finance to the purpose for which it is to be used. Do not, for example, use short-term finance for long-term investment. Do not over gear, i.e. do not take on too much fixed interest capital in relation to your own equity. A ratio of 1:1 is often required by lenders.

Keep your bank manager, accountant or other advisers involved in your plans but do not delegate too much responsibility. You must be able represent the firm in discussions with potential backers. Set your objectives and allow adequate time for planning. Your finance is likely to come from some combination of: the cash flow; the bank; 'off-balance sheet' finance; outsiders; the public or publicly-assisted sources.

Consider all sources and try to identify the best choice by making careful calculations. Make sure that you are familiar with, and understand, the special small business schemes and, if appropriate, the loan guarantee scheme.

Try not to limit your opportunities by refusing to part with equity. Many organizations are interested in minority stakes and redeemable shares may be issued.

The Business Expansion Scheme may attract sources that seek exit after five years.

If you own the freehold of your property 'sale and lease back' may be possible but professional advice is essential before taking this step.

If you are a public company not eligible for a Stock Exchange listing you can make your shares more marketable by participation in the Unlisted Securities Market.

You may be eligible for support under government or government backed schemes. Obtain and scrutinize a comprehensive summary of the many measures that are on offer.

Provide your proposed financiers with clear information, past accounts and forecasts. Supply details of your management information, accounting and budgetary systems.

Financial institutions participating in the Loan Guarantee Scheme:

| | |
|---|---|
| Allied Irish Banks | Hong Kong & Shanghai Banking Corp. |
| Bank of Credit & Commerce | Lloyds Bank |
| International | Midland Bank |
| Bank of Ireland | National Westminster Bank |
| Bank of Leumi (UK) | Northern Bank |
| Bank of Scotland | Norwich General Trust |
| Barclays Bank | Royal Bank of Scotland |
| Beneficial Trust | Standard Chartered Bank |
| British Linen Bank | Swiss Bank Corp. |
| Brown Shipley & Co. | TSB |
| Clydesdale Bank | 3i |
| Co-Operative Bank | Ulster Bank |
| Coutts & Company | United Dominions trust |
| Commercial Credit Services | Yorkshire Bank |
| County Bank | |
| Hill Samuel | |

## Appendix: How the NatWest Business Development Loan works in practice

A typical example from the NWGO portfolio would be Hibass Photomec, a small company trading from an Industrial Estate in Wellingborough, Northamptonshire.

The business was co-founded by the current Managing Director in 1971 to manufacture and sell equipment for printed circuit board production. In 1972/73 the company diversified into opto-electronic guard systems, working on an infra-red light to provide 'curtains' around dangerous machinery.

The competitive nature of the market, together with the effects of the recession in the late 1970s/early 1980s began, however, to take their toll. Consequently, the company experienced cash flow difficulties, with declining turnover and and little more than break-even being achieved.

The directors, accordingly, sought long term finance and although other offers were received they were particularly attracted to the overall package which the National Westminster Group was able to offer. The facilities made available in 1981 embraced an overdraft and a Business Development Loan as well as the Capital Loan.

An important consideration was the agreement to a two year capital and interest repayment holiday for the Capital Loan. As it turned out this proved to be of vital importance, as the company continued to experience difficulties, and by the end of 1983 the position was serious, with significant accumulated losses.

The NWGO team nevertheless reported that: 'There was a strong, clear and enthusiastic management with marketable products and with potential for continuing development'.

Accordingly, after frank discussions with the directors it was concluded that continuing sales and firm management would be the key to future success.

It was this in-depth review, which also highlighted the need to enhance certain internal records including the management accounting systems, backed up by a re-visit in November 1984, with a similarly positive outlook, that allowed NatWest to get really close to the company. The Bank was, therefore, able to continue its support when on conventional terms and considerations it would have been very difficult so to do.

NWGO's continuing faith in the management of the company was not misplaced. The management team under the dynamic leadership of Jim Bass, continued to develop new products and increase sales.

As a result, in 1984 turnover exceeded £1 million with a very satisfactory net profit being achieved.

The NWGO team has continued to maintain and to build upon the rapport established with the management and at the end of 1985 reported: 'We consider that the directors are to be congratulated on their achievements over the last four years. They have led the company from near disastrous losses to a firm base for future expansion through a swiftly changing market'.

At NWGO the Hibass story is viewed as a success. Together with assistance from the local Branch and the Area Office, the Bank's full support has been offered to the company through very difficult trading and financial conditions, based on faith in the management, the products and the market.

In the current year the company is anticipating turnover in excess of £1.2 million with commensurate profits. Meanwhile Hibass is actively pursuing the widening of its product base by means of licensing agreements, acquisitions and take-overs.

Both NWGO and the management of Hibass look forward to a continuing and developing relationship over the years to come.

*Reproduced by courtesy of National Westminster Bank PLC.*

# 10   Controlling your business

What have we done in the past? □ Evaluating and monitoring performance □ Ratios for comparison □ Budgeting □ Information systems □ Management accounting

As the owner/manager of a small business which is aiming for growth, you will need to develop a management team which is well-informed, capable of facing and overcoming business problems, and able to plan for the future success of the company. You will need to be able to survey the business activities and have an overall picture of its performance. In most small and medium-sized businesses the information available rarely presents a picture of the whole firm. Reports and other information are usually limited to financial data, which may even conceal the true position.

In previous chapters we have discussed ways of analysing and planning products, customers and markets, but to complete the picture you must look at the current and future position of the business in financial terms. Do you have a clear picture of your company's operations? An analysis of current financial information and any projected figures available should give you a better picture of what the firm's activities are achieving, and what they should yield in the future, as well as basic factors for sound economic planning.

## What have we done in the past?

We will start by looking at current and past accounts as a way of learning about the business, and identifying and evaluating options. It is important for the small firm to review how resources have been utilized, and to understand how liquidity problems can be caused by the factors which have been outlined in Chapter 8, and by other causes. Furthermore, the owners and other investors, such as the bank, will want to know what the return on their investment has been.

The profit and loss account and balance sheet are part of the complete accounts drawn up at the request of the owner/manager. All businesses should aim to have a set of accounts drawn up at least once per quarter for internal control purposes. This is relatively easy if you possess a microcomputer and one of the excellent accounting software packages now available at a reasonable cost. Such a system, besides being quick to operate, will provide a profit and loss account, a balance sheet and, if required, a set of management reports. However, a good manual double-entry book-keeping system should be capable of providing the figures for a trial balance from which a set of accounts can be prepared.

One of the aims of growth is to improve profitability, therefore it would be useful to understand profit, how it is determined and how it is affected. Businesses survive by selling things for more than they pay for them, therefore profit could be described as the difference between revenue from sales and the costs incurred by the business.

## The profit and loss account

The profit and loss account is about the past. It is a detailed statement of how costs relate to sales. The first part of the account details the trading activity, i.e. how much stock was sold, what it cost, and what it was sold for. *Gross profit* is simply the revenue from sales less the cost of the stock sold. *Net profit* is the gross profit less all the trading expenses and overheads.

The profit and loss account is merely a statement about overall trading in a previous period. If the bottom line shows a net profit, this does not mean that there is cash available, nor does it tell you how well the company is doing. The net profit needs to be measured against the capital invested, i.e. could the capital have been better invested elsewhere? The profit and loss account does not give you profit on individual items, which could mean that a loss on some products is compensated by profits on other products; nor does it tell you about long-term trends since it is for one period only.

## The balance sheet

The balance sheet is simply a statement showing the company's position on one particular day. It states where the money came from which is invested in the business at this moment. For example, sources may include some of the following:

- Capital or share capital (various types).
- Profits retained in the business, sometimes labelled 'reserves', some-times 'profit & loss account'.
- Long-term loans from various sources.
- Debentures (another sort of loan).
- Short-term loans.
- Creditors (a form of short-term loan).

● Bank overdraft (also a short-term loan).

The rest of the balance sheet merely shows how this mixture of investment has been turned into a variety of assets. For example, profits retained in the business may have been turned into vehicles or machines long before the last day of the trading year, and some of the raw material purchased from creditors may now be turned into finished goods and sitting on the shelf of a customer who owes you money, i.e. a debtor.

You are now concerned with finding out what you have done in the past and what you need to do with regard to finance and operations which will help achieve your targets. Figure 10.1 below outlines the kind of information needed for finding answers to questions on profitability, efficiency, liquidity and gearing. These terms are explained in the next section.

For the purposes of comparison and examining trends in your own business, you will need the final accounts for this year, last year and the year before. You will also need any projected profit and loss statements which have been drawn up based on the objectives laid out in the marketing plan.

| Questions | Information needed for each year |
|---|---|
| ● What is the trend on profitability? | ● Sales and cost of sales<br>● Gross profit margin<br>● Net profit margin<br>● Return on capital employed<br>● Turnover of capital employed |
| ● What is the trend on liquidity? | ● Levels of working capital<br>● Turnover of working capital<br>● Liquidity measures |
| ● What is the trend on gearing? | ● Gearing ratio<br>● Income gearing |
| ● What is the trend on efficiency? | ● Utilization of the workforce<br>● Utilization of fixed assets<br>● Utilization of other resources<br>● Overhead control |

**Fig. 10.1** Information required for questions on profitability, efficiency, liquidity and gearing

## Evaluating and monitoring performance

If we compare the most recent performance of the business with previous years, the results will indicate how the company is changing and may point to possible areas for improvement and development. By using key ratios we can examine different aspects of profitability, liquidity and efficiency. However, it is important to emphasize that a set of figures will not, on their own, provide the key to business growth. At best the figures will raise questions and provide a basis for looking more closely at highlighted areas of performance.

For the purpose of exploring each ratio you should apply them to the profit and loss accounts and balance sheets shown in Fig. 10.2. The list of key ratios and the results obtained (in figures) appear in Fig. 10.3.

The outcome is best if each ratio is applied to several sets of accounts, so that the results, if laid out in a table, will highlight trends. Such a table has been prepared for your own use in the action list at the end of this chapter. Before applying any ratios simply study the figures and aim to get a 'feel' for the situation. Your knowledge of your own business, and a degree of intuition, can add substance and meaning to trends and indications suggested by the bare figures.

In the case study, *Status Engineering* (Fig. 10.2), a general study of the figures, without applying any ratios, tells you the following:

- Upward trend in sales. £100,000 – £120,000 – £150,000
- Profit levels up before and after tax.
- Significant increase in plant.
- Significant increase in stock levels, especially in year 3.
- A greater proportion of net profits is retained each year: £1,400 (17.5%), £2,800 (25.9%), £5,000 (33.3%).
- Significant increase in borrowing, i.e. from no loans in year 1 to high loans in year 3.
- No actual cash in year 3.
- Turnover up 50% overall, but capital employed up 150%.
  ('Capital employed' is the amount of money invested in the business; it is owners' equity plus long-term loans from any source.)

The observations will give rise to a number of questions. At first glance there are many factors in this business which would cause concern to the potential investor, e.g. the relationship of capital employed to turnover. In the first year capital employed of £40,000 achieves sales of £100,000, but by the third year capital employed has increased to £105,000 and sales achieved have only risen to £150,000. The increase in plant might be an indication of greater efficiency, but so far it has had little effect on sales and profits, and has caused an extensive increase in borrowing. Levels of stock held have increased in relation to sales, suggesting that working capital is lying idle on the shelves. The general picture is one of gloom. But the owner of the business has greater knowledge. We need to know why the

*Status Engineering Ltd – Financial Statement*

|  | Year 1 £ | Year 2 £ | Year 3 £ |
|---|---|---|---|
| Sales turnover | 100,000 | 120,000 | 150,000 |
| *Less* cost of sales | (60,000) | (70,000) | (87,000) |
| *Gross profit* | 40,000 | 50,000 | 63,000 |
| Less overheads | (32,000) | (39,200) | (48,000) |
| Net profit before tax & dividends | 8,000 | 10,800 | 15,000 |
| Net profit after tax & dividends | 1,400 | 2,800 | 5,000 |

*The Balance Sheet of Status Engineering Ltd – Last three years*

|  | Year 1 |  | Year 2 |  | Year 3 |  |
|---|---|---|---|---|---|---|
| Ordinary share capital | 30,000 |  | 30,000 |  | 30,000 |  |
| *Plus* reserves | 10,000 | 40,000 | 12,800 | 42,800 | 17,800 | 47,800 |
| Loan capital from various sources |  | – |  | 22,000 |  | 57,200 |
|  |  | 40,000 |  | 64,800 |  | 105,000 |
| Plant original cost | 27,000 |  | 50,000 |  | 70,000 |  |
| *Less* depreciation | (7,000) | 20,000 | (10,800) | 39,200 | (15,000) | 55,000 |
| Stocks | 20,000 |  | 30,000 |  | 50,000 |  |
| Debtors | 20,000 |  | 22,000 |  | 25,000 |  |
| Cash | 4,000 | 44,000 | 2,000 | 54,000 | – | 75,000 |
|  |  | 64,000 |  | 93,200 |  | 130,000 |
| *Less* current liabilities Creditors |  | (24,000) |  | (28,400) |  | (25,000) |
|  |  | 40,000 |  | 64,800 |  | 105,000 |

**Fig. 10.2**

10

business has tooled up and taken the risk of such large borrowings. Are there areas of inefficiency? Can they be identified? What are the prospects for the business, and most significantly, *what is in the order book?*

Now you should look at the figures from the ratio analysis, Fig. 10.3, to help concentrate your thinking, and perhaps raise more specific questions which will aid the investigations.

## Return on capital employed (ROCE)

This is probably the most important ratio since it tells all the investors, i.e. shareholders, owners, banks and other lenders, how well their money is performing. It measures net profit as percentage of capital employed, just as you would measure the rate of interest gained from money invested in a building society account. Status Engineering shows an alarming decrease, from 20 per cent down to 14.2 per cent: it confirms our fears that total sales have not increased in proportion to the investment. A further measure of profitability is to discover how often the capital employed turns over within the financial year. This ratio shows a similar declining trend, moving from 2.5 to 1.43 times. You must ask a number of questions:

- Why has this business borrowed £57,200?
- Is this decline temporary, having been caused by borrowing so that the business can prepare for a take-off?
- What are the proposals in the business plan put forward to the lenders? What is the time scale for achieving them?
- Has demand fallen off? Where are the products on the product life cycle? Is there some form of diversification?

For a limited company a ROCE of 20 per cent would be reasonably healthy since salaries have been paid before arriving at the net profit figure. In the case of Status Engineering, the lenders may feel concern at a ROCE of 14.2 per cent in year 3; however, the shareholders, whose own investment is less than half of the capital employed, may regard the picture differently since they would not have the opportunity to invest the borrowed £57,200 elsewhere.

For a sole trader or partnership the ROCE would have to be measured after an appropriate figure for drawings had been deducted from net profit.

## Gross margin

Gross margin is gross profit measured against sales and expressed as a percentage. For a manufacturer, gross margin is the most significant ratio.

| | Year 1 | Year 2 | Year 3 |
|---|---|---|---|
| Return on capital employed: | | | |
| $\dfrac{\text{Net profit before tax}}{\text{Capital employed}}$ % | 20% | 16.66% | 14.28% |
| $\dfrac{\text{Gross profit}}{\text{Sales}}$ % | 40% | 41.66% | 42% |
| $\dfrac{\text{Net profit}}{\text{Sales}}$ % | 8% | 9% | 10% |
| $\dfrac{\text{Overheads}}{\text{Sales}}$ % | 32% | 32.66% | 32% |
| Capital employed turnover: | | | |
| $\dfrac{\text{Sales}}{\text{Capital employed}}$ = No. times | 2.5 | 1.85 | 1.43 |
| Stockturn: | | | |
| $\dfrac{\text{Cost of sales}}{\text{Stock}}$ = Times | 3 | 2.3 | 1.74 |
| Credit given: | | | |
| $\dfrac{\text{Sales}}{\text{Debtors}}$ × 365 = No. days | 73 | 67 | 61 |
| Working capital levels | £20,000 | £25,600 | £50,000 |
| Current assets : current liabilities | 1.83 : 1 | 1.9 : 1 | 3 : 1 |
| Acid test | 1 : 1 | 0.85 : 1 | 1 : 1 |
| Working capital turnover: | | | |
| $\dfrac{\text{Sales}}{\text{Working capital}}$ = No. times | 5 | 4.68 | 3 |
| Gearing: | | | |
| Loans : equity | – | 0.51:1 | 1.19:1 |

**10**

**Fig. 10.3**

There must be enough gross profit to cover all of the overheads, salaries, drawings, and finance costs, as well as to create sufficient levels of cash for loan repayments, and to allow some for reinvestment in the business. In most cases gross margin is the same as 'contribution' which is discussed in detail in Chapter 7.

## Net margin

This is the net profit figure before tax and dividends, measured as a percentage of sales. For every business there is a norm. For example, a service industry would expect a very high net margin, and a nuts and bolts manufacturer would expect a low one, but the level of overall sales would be considerably higher for the latter if they were to achieve the same profits.

Status Engineering shows that profits appear to be increasing. At first glance this seems to conflict with the ROCE which suggests that the business is not doing so well. What, then, is net margin? In this case it actually tells us that each £1 of sales has yielded more pence in the pound each year, while ROCE indicates that there were simply not enough total sales. Again there are a number of questions which may add to the picture.

- Have prices increased? Has demand dropped?
- Have costs reduced? Better buying? More streamlined production?
- Has the product changed? Is it a new product at the introduction stage?
- Is there a marketing problem?

## Efficiency

Perhaps a look at the efficiency of this business will throw some light on our continuing concern. Any cost shown in the profit and loss account can be measured against sales. For instance, *cost of materials* to sales will tell you something about more or less efficient usage or better buying. The same applies to *labour* and *overheads*. Three important indicators will be considered specifically.

## Rate of stockturn

High levels of stock can mean that working capital is not being used efficiently. By dividing the cost of sales by the average stock held throughout the year, we can measure how often stock turns over. The more often it turns over the more often it generates profits.

For Status Engineering the trend is very definitely downward. In a small engineering company a stockturn of 4 or 5 times a year is about the norm, and for other industries it will be very different. For example, a fishmonger may need to turn over stock every few days.

For this company there are two important questions:

- Does the stock figure used in the ratio represent the true 'average stock' held throughout year 3? (The figure used is shown in the balance sheet.)
- Has there been a stock piling exercise towards the end of the third year? Is this in line with the tooling up which is aimed at new production levels in year 4?

## Credit given

You want to know whether this business has been borrowing funds to cover a credit control problem which would otherwise seriously affect cash flow. This ratio has also been mentioned in Chapter 8 with regard to the control of working capital. It would appear that Status Engineering is becoming more efficient, having reduced its period of collection to 61 days, a norm for the industry.

## Credit taken

A similar ratio will reveal how long the company takes, on average, to pay its bills. This will give indications about cash flow and likely relationships with suppliers.

10

## Liquidity

Lenders and suppliers are particularly interested in how well a company can cover its day-to-day costs, which are met out of working capital. A business with insufficient levels of such capital, or which is inefficient in its use of it, may become illiquid, i.e. unable to meet its bills as they occur.

## Current ratio

By measuring current assets as a ratio against current liabilities we can see how well the business can cover each £1 owed. The following information helps.

The level of working capital = current assets *less* current liabilities
Current assets = stock, debtors, bank, cash
Current liabilities = creditors, overdraft, short-term loans

In the case of Status Engineering there is £1.83 in the first year, £1.90 in the second, and £3 in the third available to cover every £1 of debt. This is extremely healthy – despite there being no real cash in the third year!

## Acid test

However, the equation has included stock, thus making the assumption that stock can be quickly turned into cash for paying the bills. Stock in many industries is extremely vulnerable, e.g. in the fashion trade stock can quickly lose its value, so it would be interesting to see if the bills can still be covered if this item were taken out of the sum. This is known as the 'acid test' – can they pay at the crunch? The figures show that Status has no liquidity problems at all since 1:1 is an ideal ratio.

## Working capital turnover

Like stock, the working capital needs to turn over as often as possible in order to generate profits. A sudden increase in working capital in the third year has affected the rate of turnover; this relates to the increase in stock levels. The same questions apply here as for stockturn.

## Gearing ratios

Finally, the business must be concerned with the balance of equity to loans (this has also been emphasized in the previous chapter). The higher the borrowing, the greater the responsibility for interest and loan repayment. These payments will affect the cash flow and therefore must be budgeted for well in advance. The first gearing ratio simply measures the relationship of loans to equity. In Status there are no loans in the first year, in the second they borrow at the rate of 0.52:1, or 52 per cent, and in the third year loans increase to 1.19:1, or 119 per cent of owners' equity.

Since the amount of borrowing has risen so dramatically it is important that the business can generate sufficient profits to cover the interest payments, as well as leave funds for other purposes, including any actual loan repayments. In this case a measurement of net profit before tax and interest, divided by the interest payable, will tell you how well interest is covered. The answer needs to be that interest is covered at least twice.

These ratios are important when considering how you will finance your business expansion. They have been discussed in the previous chapter in this context.

## Conclusions

The initial picture presented by the figures for Status Engineering has changed. There are a number of questions about the forward plans, order book and product which need further investigation. Indications are that this company is gearing up for expansion early in the next period.

As stated earlier, however, the ratios do not give answers – they raise searching questions. Used constructively and intuitively they can assist greatly in monitoring, controlling and evaluating your business.

You will probably agree that the case study would have been greatly enhanced had the projected figures for year 4 been put alongside the previous years, together with an outline of the complete business plan for the next period. This highlights the value of planning ahead.

Increased profitability means gaining an overall increase in the return on capital employed (ROCE). A small business may have weaknesses in one or several areas which can be highlighted by the use of ratios. An interesting way of looking at the weaknesses (and strengths) is to see how they fit into the pyramid of ratios shown in Fig. 10.4. Each leg of the pyramid shows a route for strengthening the ROCE. A business owner/manager can often identify whole areas in the business where better controls would directly affect overall performance.

## Ratios for comparison

10

If yours is a limited company then your suppliers and competitors will have access to your accounts and can apply these ratios. You should regularly assess your customers, your competitors and some of your suppliers in the same way. Most larger companies undertake this exercise as a matter of course, and your business has probably already been researched by more than one.

It is useful to assess your own company by comparing it with your competitors, and with the industry norms. However, many small businesses are unique and such comparisons are impractical. Most trade associations can provide useful statistics for this kind of exercise. The following addresses may also prove helpful:

---

| | |
|---|---|
| Companies Registration Office Crown Way, Maindy, Cardiff CF4 | – all companies must file records with the government |
| | – any company accounts are available on microfiche for a small charge |
| 102 George Street Edinburgh EH2 | – most libraries have a microfiche reader |

|  |  |
|---|---|
|  | – many libraries will obtain information for you |
| Centre for Interfirm Comparison | – founded by the BIM |
| 25 Bloomsbury Square | – may have reports for particular |
| London WC1A 2PJ | trade associations |
|  | – firms supply information on their own company performance, and receive information on similar firms |
|  | – individual company performance is confidential |
| ICC Business Ratios | – sector reports analysing performance |
| 23 City Road | over a three year period |
| London EC1Y 1AA | – ratios, industry norms, trends |
|  | – 150 different industry sectors |

## Budgeting

A budget is a statement of your plans for the business. Once the longer term plans have been designed, budgets are simply ways of translating them into operational commitments for shorter time periods. You may remember the reference to budgets in Chapter 5 when discussing the marketing plan.

Most budgets are divided into four-weekly or calendar month periods. Each sector of the business will need a budget, therefore the whole management team must be involved in designing the targets and activities for each period. Those responsible for departments or sections of the business should develop the finer details of their own budgets, using information from those involved in the section and taking into consideration the strengths and weaknesses of the resources available.

A microcomputer spreadsheet package makes the whole exercise much simpler. It saves a considerable amount of time by taking away the tedium of lengthy sums. But more important, it allows for updating and rapid change should sudden opportunities appear. It also makes it easier to carry out sensitivity analyses, i.e. testing 'what-if' situations. If you do not have a computer perhaps you should budget for one now! An example form for budgeting, in this case for overheads, is shown in Fig. 10.5.

### The cash budget

Most small firms have prepared a cash budget (or cash flow forecast), as part of the original start-up plan. Over a period of years the majority develop their own system of budgeting for cash levels. Regular forecasts should be drawn up at least quarterly in a growing situation. Monthly

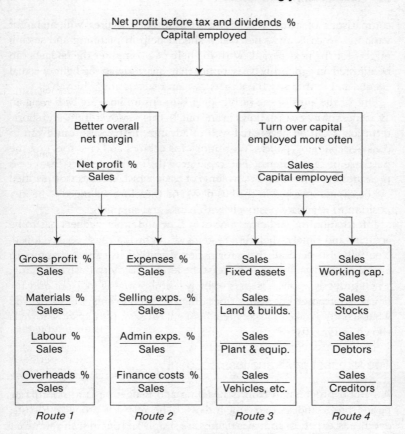

Fig. 10.4 Strengthening the return on capital employed

comparisons of actual results with the forecast figures will highlight variances in costs and sales which should help in planning and setting targets for the next period. With the help of a computer the budgets can be adjusted on a monthly basis, rather than quarterly, in the light of actual events, and in this way the targets remain realistic and achievable.

One of the aims of the cash budget is to ensure liquidity by having an awareness of *when* cash flows in and out. In this way overdrafts and short-term loans can be negotiated well in advance. It may also cause you to consider changing policies on timings for debtors and creditors and the purchase of capital items. The rapid growth firm may suffer from cash pressures brought about by a volume of trade which exceeds that justified by the capital invested in the business, and therefore will need to be in a position to negotiate positively with banks and suppliers.

Information for updating your cash flow and other budgets has to be accurate and timely, therefore systems of reporting must be developed. You will also need all the information discussed in earlier chapters to enable you and your team to forecast the levels of activity. Cash budgeting, when properly applied, is an extremely useful planning tool, not only for liquidity purposes but also for deciding on when events will occur, and what actions to take to make them happen. An example cash flow form is shown in Fig. 10.6.

## The forecast profit and loss account

A natural progression from scheduling and budgeting is a monthly or period profit and loss account forecast. The relevant production costs, overheads, expenses and sales figures are simply laid out in such a way that the outcome of trading can be assessed on a monthly basis. A profit and loss forecast form is shown in Fig. 10.7. Again, information on costs, stock levels, prices and overheads must be readily available.

## Information systems

### Orders, enquiries and complaints

It is vital to ensure that there is a recording system for both orders and enquiries. This will help monitor customer requirements and the firm's ability to capture business. Every enquiry is a potential sale, so a follow-up procedure needs to be established and the results recorded.

Many firms are poor at handling complaints. This is a sure way of losing valuable customers. Many firms adopt a policy of encouraging customers to complain; in this way they can communicate by demonstrating to the

| Overheads | Prev. Year | Actual | Forecast | Jan | Feb | Mar | Apr | May | June | July | Aug | Sept | Oct | Nov | Dec |
|---|---|---|---|---|---|---|---|---|---|---|---|---|---|---|---|
| (a) *Manufacturing* Rent, Rates Transport Machine Repairs Heat & Light Depr. Machinery | | | | | | | | | | | | | | | |
| (b) *Selling* Salaries, NHI, etc. Discounts Comm. paid Bad Debts Travel Printing, Stationery Adverts. Depr. Vehicles | | | | | | | | | | | | | | | |
| (c) *Administration* Insurance Postages Audit Fees Cleaning Depr. Furniture, etc. | | | | | | | | | | | | | | | |
| (d) *Finance* Bank Int. Loan Int. Leasing HP | | | | | | | | | | | | | | | |

**Fig. 10.5** Overheads budget

10

| | Jan | Feb | Mar | Apr | May | June | July | Aug | Sept | Oct | Nov | Dec | Total | |
|---|---|---|---|---|---|---|---|---|---|---|---|---|---|---|
| *Cash Receipts* | | | | | | | | | | | | | | |
| Cash Sales | | | | | | | | | | | | | | |
| Debtors | | | | | | | | | | | | | | |
| VAT (Net receipt) | | | | | | | | | | | | | | |
| Other income | | | | | | | | | | | | | | |
| Sale of Assets | | | | | | | | | | | | | | |
| Other Receipts | | | | | | | | | | | | | | |
| TOTAL    A | | | | | | | | | | | | | | |
| Opening Bank (Cr) | | | | | | | | | | | | | | |
| TOTAL B | | | | | | | | | | | | | | |
| *Cash Payments* | | | | | | | | | | | | | | |
| Materials – Cash | | | | | | | | | | | | | | |
| Credit Purchases | | | | | | | | | | | | | | |
| Wages | | | | | | | | | | | | | | |
| Overheads | | | | | | | | | | | | | | |
| Taxation | | | | | | | | | | | | | | |
| VAT (Net Payment) | | | | | | | | | | | | | | |
| Capital Expenditure | | | | | | | | | | | | | | |
| Loan Repayments | | | | | | | | | | | | | | |
| HP/Leasing interest costs | | | | | | | | | | | | | | |
| Bank Interest | | | | | | | | | | | | | | |
| TOTAL    C | | | | | | | | | | | | | | |
| Opening Bank (Dr.) | | | | | | | | | | | | | | |
| TOTAL D | | | | | | | | | | | | | | |

* Difference between B & D

* Carry forward to next column against A or C

**Fig. 10.6** Cash flow forecast

**Fig. 10.7** Profit and loss account forecast

| | Prev. Year | Actual | Forecast | Jan | Feb | Mar | Apr | May | June | July | Aug | Sept | Oct | Nov | Dec |
|---|---|---|---|---|---|---|---|---|---|---|---|---|---|---|---|
| *Sales* | | | | | | | | | | | | | | | |
| Cash | | | | | | | | | | | | | | | |
| Credit | | | | | | | | | | | | | | | |
| *Cost of Sales* | | | | | | | | | | | | | | | |
| Cash | | | | | | | | | | | | | | | |
| Credit | | | | | | | | | | | | | | | |
| Wages | | | | | | | | | | | | | | | |
| * Stock Adjustment | | | | | | | | | | | | | | | |
| Direct Costs | | | | | | | | | | | | | | | |
| Gross Profit % | | | | | | | | | | | | | | | |
| *Overheads* | | | | | | | | | | | | | | | |
| Manufacturing | | | | | | | | | | | | | | | |
| Selling | | | | | | | | | | | | | | | |
| Administration | | | | | | | | | | | | | | | |
| Drawings | | | | | | | | | | | | | | | |
| Operating Profit % | | | | | | | | | | | | | | | |
| Miscell. (Net) | | | | | | | | | | | | | | | |
| Finance Charges | | | | | | | | | | | | | | | |
| Profit before Tax | | | | | | | | | | | | | | | |
| * Opening Stock less | | | | | | | | | | | | | | | |
| Closing Stock | | | | | | | | | | | | | | | |

10

customer that he or she is much valued. Complaints handling should be delegated to a competent, sympathetic individual, and there should be procedures for recording them and monitoring the outcome.

- Are all enquiries, estimates and quotations recorded?
- What is the conversion rate from enquiries, etc., to sales?
- Is there a procedure for reviewing and following up enquiries?
- What is the order mix? Does it fit the budgets?
- What is the time scale from order to delivery?
- How many orders are outstanding?
- How many complaints have been received?
- How many of the outcomes were satisfactory from the customer's point of view?

## Sales and credit control

Your present systems for invoicing are probably adequate. However, it may be necessary to review the types of stationery used and the capability of the system to move at a quicker rate. Carbonated, three- and four-part stationery can be used manually and in computerized systems, and can save repetition and the mistakes that often go with transferring information. Ensuring that delivery notes go with the goods and that invoices are dispatched the same day (instead of monthly as is the practice in some businesses) will mean that you can send a statement out at the end of the month.

Sales need to be recorded in a system, Day Book or computer, which analyses items such as VAT, but it would be even more useful if the system also analysed the sales mix.

Credit control has been discussed at length in Chapter 8. It is only necessary to remind you of the need for good recording systems which will yield information on debtors and creditors, and provide an aged debtors list.

## Costing and pricing

When a product or service involves any combination of manpower, materials and technology, each component must be costed and the information captured. Many firms fail to apply any type of costing criteria and consequently, as the business grows and jobs become more complex, they find costing has become a major problem, often resulting in inaccurate pricing and profitless exercises.

Before you take your business into the next phase, examine your systems for costing and pricing.

- Can you identify fixed costs?
- Do you know the contributions of each product/service?
- Which are the most profitable products?
- How frequently do you check the costs of overheads?
- Is labour and machine efficiency regularly reviewed?
- Can you identify the amount of scrap? Are scrap levels too high?
- How many items have to be reworked?
- How do you control overtime? How is it costed?

## Stock control

Holding stock ties up working capital and affects liquidity. If you are about to increase your buying levels to meet the anticipated growth in sales then ensure that a good recording system is installed which will identify fast- and slow-moving items, and provide figures for levels of individual stocks.

You will also need to have a source of information for the following:

- Quarterly valuation of stock at cost.
- Information on alternative sources of supply, and contacts by name.
- Information on current suppliers.
- Discounts available, size of required orders, etc.
- Order levels and times.
- Storage details, needs for different products, layout of store, etc.

## Basic records

The basic records in many small firms often consist of an analysed cash book and two files, one for unpaid and the other for paid invoices. This system is often adequate when the business is very small, especially since the owner/manager usually wears a number of hats including that of book-keeper. In a growth situation, however, where much more informa-tion is required, such recording procedures are totally inadequate. The business will now need a full double-entry book-keeping system. This includes cash books, various day books, purchase, sales, and nominal ledgers.

Monthly totals and balances are required, and the cash situation should be reviewed weekly or monthly, and even daily in some crucial situations. The cash book must be updated and reconciled to the bank statements at least monthly and the company cash balance will be more up-to-date than the bank statement.

## Asset register

From the start of a business all assets purchased and disposed of should be recorded, at cost and by the date purchased. These can be grouped under headings such as 'motor vehicles', 'plant & equipment', 'fixtures & fittings', etc. A note of the depreciation charged for each item, a figure usually set by your accountant, can be entered alongside.

Besides the normal taxation implications, you will want to assess performance against the cost of holding the asset.

## Profit and loss account and balance sheet

A well kept book-keeping system, totalled and balanced each month, should be capable of producing a trial balance which is suitable for interim accounts. This means using these figures, along with the stock figure, to produce a profit and loss account for the purpose of monitoring the company's progress.

Historical accounts presented three months after the end of the financial year for tax purposes are insufficient for business control since they appear long after the action, although they do have a place in forward planning exercises.

## Management accounting

A small company may not be able to afford the services of a management accountant too often, but a system can be set up where, if regular profit and loss accounts are produced, the figures can be used to draw comparisons between different periods, and even with different companies, using the ratios and methods outlined earlier in this chapter.

Many computerized accounting packages automatically produce profit and loss accounts, balance sheets, and a set of management reports with ratios. These packages are based on the same principles as a manual system, but the actual task of recording is significantly more simple. In addition, there are spreadsheet packages which are ideal for designing your own budget layouts, and which do all the sums for you. Spreadsheets appear to have endless applications. A database package is reasonably cheap to add to a system, and it provides a simple means of storing, sifting and retrieving data, such as lists of names, stores records, etc.

A simple management reporting system would provide information at regular intervals, such as:

- Gross and net margins, i.e. what percentage of the sales is profit.
- Comparisons of expenses for each period.
- Measurement of net profit against the total capital invested in the business.
- The break-even. Information gathered on fixed and variable costs (e.g. direct labour and materials) and pricing can be used to calculate the sales needed in a certain period to cover all the outgoings.
- Trends for all of these items – this should help with sales forecasting.
- Forecasts on the capacity of production, distribution, and administration, which will be important elements or limiting factors in forecasting sales and budgeting.

---

1. Before applying ratios to your accounts look at the figures and make notes on the general impressions gained.
2. Use the table on the next page to evaluate the past, current and projected performance of your company.
3. Examine your recording procedures in detail and assess where improvements could be introduced. If you do not have a computerized system start researching the cost of putting one in. A good starting place for unbiased advice is your local college.

**10**

|  | Year before last | Last year | This year | Next year |
|---|---|---|---|---|
| *Profitability*<br>1. Return on capital<br>   employed (ROCE)<br><br>   $\dfrac{\text{Net profit before tax \& div.}}{\text{Capital employed}}$ % |  |  |  |  |
| 2. Gross margin<br><br>   $\dfrac{\text{Gross profit}}{\text{Sales}}$ % |  |  |  |  |
| 3. Net margin<br><br>   $\dfrac{\text{Net margin}}{\text{Sales}}$ % |  |  |  |  |
| *Efficiency*<br><br>4. $\dfrac{\text{Costs of materials}}{\text{Sales}}$ % |  |  |  |  |
| 5. $\dfrac{\text{Cost of labour}}{\text{Sales}}$ % |  |  |  |  |
| 6. $\dfrac{\text{Overhead costs}}{\text{Sales}}$ % |  |  |  |  |
| 7. $\dfrac{\text{Sales}}{\text{Fixed assets}}$ = No. times |  |  |  |  |
| 8. $\dfrac{\text{Debtors}}{\text{Sales}} \times 365$ = No. days |  |  |  |  |

|  | Year before last | Last year | This year | Next year |
|---|---|---|---|---|
| 9. $\dfrac{\text{Creditors}}{\text{Purchases}} \times 365 = \text{No. days}$ |  |  |  |  |
| 10. Stockturn<br><br>$\dfrac{\text{Cost of sales}}{\text{Stock}} = \text{No. times}$ |  |  |  |  |
| *Liquidity*<br><br>11. Working capital levels<br>Current assets – current liabilities |  |  |  |  |
| 12. Current ratio<br>Current assets: current liabilities |  |  |  |  |
| 13. Acid test<br>Current assets<br>*Less* stock : current liabilities |  |  |  |  |
| 14. Working capital turnover<br><br>$\dfrac{\text{Sales}}{\text{Working capital}} = \text{No. times.}$ |  |  |  |  |
| *Gearing*<br><br>15. Loans: equity |  |  |  |  |
| 16. Income gearing<br><br>$\dfrac{\text{Short-term loans + interest}}{\text{Interest}}$ |  |  |  |  |

10

# 11 Legal aspects of growth

Should you take a partner? □ Should you incorporate as a private limited liability company? □ Consumer credit □ Increasing the authorized share capital and/or amending the memorandum of association □ Forms of contract □ Selling techniques new to the firm □ Purchasing an existing business □ New product, process, material or mechanism

The starting points and routes related to growth are varied. As a result the legal implications of growth as they affect your firm may be very different to those currently confronting other readers. A full account of such matters is beyond the scope of this book but all business owners need to keep abreast of the law. They should not put their growth and their firm at risk by failing to pursue the right enquiries, set up the right mechanisms, or recognize when advice is needed. Consequently your attention is drawn to a selection of growth related issues, some of which, addressed during the start-up process, now have to be reconsidered. The list is not exhaustive and little is said about employment matters but you are strongly advised to read a companion book in this series, *Hiring and Firing* by Karen Lanz, which includes an excellent guide to employment law.

Will your growth plans affect the form of your business?

## Should you take a partner?

You will have, in all probability, previously decided to run your business as sole trader, partnership or limited liability company. If growth for you means converting from sole trader to a partnership, professional advice should be sought. Undoubtedly your adviser will emphasize the need for a partnership agreement. You will also be told that each partner is liable without limit for all the debts of the firm. You will be liable for your partner even though he or she may not have consulted you. Your partner(s) could make you bankrupt. Clearly they must be chosen with great care. Your accountant may advise you that your incoming partners should pay you a sum for the goodwill that you have created but in which they now participate.

## Partnership checklist

---

1. Do you need the partner(s) for expertise, additional finance or some other reason?
2. Have you considered other ways of acquiring the expertise, finance or dealing with the 'other reasons'?
3. Have you assessed the goodwill value of your business for the purposes of payment to you by incoming partners?
4. Given your exposure to unlimited liability satisfy yourself as to the degree of trust that can be placed in your proposed partner(s).
5. Seek advice on partnership assurance to safeguard you and your partners against any premature death that would deprive the firm of withdrawn funds. Such an assurance could be linked with pension arrangements.
6. Get advice from your solicitor on a partnership agreement.
7. The agreement should cover, *inter alia*, the following:
   (a) profit sharing;
   (b) drawings and the extent to which interest is payable on overdrawn accounts;
   (c) interest on capital;
   (d) retirement provisions;
   (e) admission of new partners;
   (f) removal of existing partners;
   (g) role and duties of individual partners;
   (h) voting rights;
   (i) procedures for running the bank account, accounting and auditing.

11

---

## Should you incorporate as a private limited liability company?

This question often arises at the growth stage. Again professional advice is essential. A company can be purchased cheaply 'off the shelf' or your solicitor can create a 'tailor-made' company. Whether you should incorporate depends upon such issues as the projected size of the business, the risks of the business and how they are affected by expansion, raising additional finance and tax matters.

If expansion means greater investment in fixed assets and an increase in the break-even point the firm is more vulnerable when demand falls off and is difficult to predict. This in itself may be sufficient to cause the owners to seek the protection of limited liability enabling them to separate personal wealth from business finances. Such protection may also be prompted when any form of diversification carries greater risk than the existing range of activities. An Avon-based restaurateur took this step when launching into the entertainment business which required him to book expensive acts and premises well in advance. The protection granted by incorporation is effective against trade credit (although some of your suppliers may use a 'Romalpa' clause under which they may acquire the right to the return of their supplies not yet paid for at a time of insolvency. This device is more to the detriment of other creditors than you). The protection for small business owners may be removed by banks and landlords who seek personal guarantees from you and/or your co-owners.

Your decision to incorporate may be driven by your need to raise additional finance required for expansion. In practice only companies, for whom raising finance is easier than for unincorporated firms, can create a floating charge. This device gives the lender security against all assets of the company including the stock. The floating charge does not prevent the company from buying and selling its assets in the normal way.

Easier access to finance also arises because there are people who are willing to invest in business but do not wish to work in them. In particular, limited liability status is a prerequisite for the funds that may become available as a result of the Business Expansion Scheme (see pages 106–7). Outside investment may come from institutional investors (e.g. 3i's – Investors in Industry plc) and, for some, the Unlisted Securities Market may beckon. Where and how you raise the outside money will have important implications for your business. Some institutions, most notably venture capital funds, will want a say in the management of the business by means of a seat on the board, others will not. In any event in issuing shares the business owner will have to make decisions as to the extent to which he wishes to retain control (51% of the shares). Some independence may have to be sacrificed if growth is the all important goal and can only be achieved with greater tranches of equity capital.

Incorporation to facilitate growth may create the opportunity to motivate employees 'key' to the growth process. They could be issued with shares through an approved employee share scheme which leads to beneficial tax treatment.

The number of persons permitted to be directors in a private company (whose shares can only be transferred with the agreement of the members) is limited to 50, but few companies will have more than 20, the maximum number (subject to exceptions such as solicitors) in a partnership, so most readers will be choosing between a partnership and private limited liability company. The disadvantages of incorporation relate to the loss of privacy as accounts have to be published, increased bureaucracy and the costs of complying with legislation. Also your wages as a director will be subject to PAYE and there will be increased national insurance costs. In addition you lose some flexibility in using the firm's money. Loans to directors in excess of £2,500 are prohibited by the Companies Act 1985.

Partnerships (and sole traders) pay tax on all profits including retained profits. The highest rate of income tax is 40% (September 1989). In a limited company as a director you will pay tax on earnings as an employee but retained profits will attract only corporation tax (25% for smaller companies). As the top rates of income tax have been reduced, the required level of profits at which incorporation becomes attractive has increased. Your accountant will advise you but for taxation reasons alone incorporation is not attractive unless each person sharing profits receives about £27,000 per year.

## The legal aspects of incorporation checklist

---

1. Have you carefully assessed the amount of finance required for expansion?
2. What effect will raising outside finance have on your control of the business?
3. Will outside investors require a seat on the board? If so, what expertise will they bring?
4. Will outsiders require dividends and, if so, will this be in conflict with your own desire to keep profits in the business? If so, can preferred ordinary shares be issued to guarantee them a dividend while not committing you to a dividend to ordinary shareholders?
5. Have you given due consideration to:
   (a) the size of the company;
   (b) the taxation position;
   (c) the costs of incorporation and compliance with legislation;
   (d) lack of flexibility in using the firm's money;
   (e) status and participation of 'key' employees;
   (f) the requirements of banks and others for personal guarantees?
6. Are you aware of your responsibilities as a director? (Leading accountants publish free of charge useful booklets.)
   (a) You must act in 'good faith' and with skill and care.
   (b) Your powers are described in the company's Articles of Association.
   (c) If you permit the company to trade while insolvent, you may be personally liable for the debts arising.
7. Be aware of other sources of personal liability and enquire about a directors' and officers' liability insurance.

---

## Does growth mean that you will now be giving consumer credit?

If your route to expansion is to enlarge sales by introducing consumer credit (instalments and hire-purchase), you will need a licence as required by the Consumer Credit Act 1974. You will not require a licence for ordinary trading where customers are given a month or so to pay. You are also exempt if you (a) give credit to limited companies and (b) enter into transactions of £30 or less with partnerships and sole traders. If consumer credit applies to you get advice from your local Trading Standards Officer.

## If you already have a company, do you need to increase the authorized share capital and/or amend the memorandum of association?

If you wish to increase the authorized share capital you will need to pass an ordinary resolution (i.e. 50% of the votes or more) but remember to follow the correct procedures. Your solicitor or accountant will be able to advise you. Your company's memorandum of association sets out the company's objectives and if your proposed expansion, perhaps based on diversification, goes outside the range of activities described in the objects clause then you will need a special resolution (75% of the votes or more) at a shareholders meeting. Much will depend on the breadth of your current memorandum and the nature of the proposed changes. Life will be complicated for you if you make contracts beyond the powers of the company and so it becomes important to follow the correct legal procedures.

## Will growth change the nature or form of contracts that you enter into?

Expansion may bring new customers and/or suppliers and even a change in the strength of your bargaining position. You may already be accustomed to trading on the standard contract terms of your suppliers and customers. Smaller firms often find themselves in a 'take it or leave it' situation with no opportunity to negotiate the terms but that is not to say that even very small firms do not sometimes issue their own terms. This is most likely to arise when they are dealing with consumers. (A light haulier in Worcester used his own standard form which was never questioned by private consumers but when contracting with a large retail concern for valuable work they decided the terms.)

As you grow your opportunities to prevail may increase and growth increases the need for standard term contracts. If you are new to standard contracts then acquaint yourself with the Unfair Contract Terms Act 1977 and the law generally relating to exemption clauses and indemnity clauses. Suffice it to say here if you deal with someone on your own standard written terms any attempt by you to avoid liability for breach of contract (or substitute an alternative performance) will only be enforceable if satisfying the test of 'reasonableness'. (The Act gives guidance on this test but you will find your local Trading Standards Officer prepared to give advice and provide you with useful booklets on the topic.)

Incidentally, there are severe restrictions on firms in seeking to use exemption clauses when dealing with consumers.

## Will expansion be based on increased sales through selling techniques new to the firm?

If this is so ensure that your proposed selling methods do not attract the disapproval of the law. You should avoid 'inertia selling' (unsolicited goods). This involves sending unsolicited goods with an invoice. The relevant legislation is the Unsolicited Goods and Services Act 1975 and the Unsolicited Goods and Services (Invoices, etc.) Regulations 1975.

Pyramid selling is also unacceptable. It is direct selling through a pyramid of distributors, each of whom sells to someone at a lower tier. Eventually those at the bottom are saddled with high prices and unwanted goods. Regulations under the Fair Trading Act 1973 have abolished the worst aspects of this form of selling. It would be unsound to base any business expansion on anything resembling this technique.

## Will expansion be based on some form of mail order?

A sports shop in Sheffield achieved growth by selling running shoes through advertisements in running magazines with a nationwide circulation. Mail order can clearly be an excellent way to reach new markets and expand but unfortunately, as Roger Cook's *Checkpoint* has shown all too often, the system can be abused to the detriment of the customer. Consequently if you are, for the first time, about to go in this direction, there are legal as well as commercial considerations.

Commercially you must have good target marketing, good image and reputation and good service. All of this needs to be underpinned by a mechanism that avoids legal pitfalls. Your advertisements and mail shots should be so drawn that they fall short of being an offer, i.e. a statement that will commit you to a contract when the 'customer' responds. It is better for you if these responses carry the status of 'invitation to treat' and this can be achieved by careful wording including statements such as 'subject to availability when the reply is received'. This becomes a safeguard so that where a supplier lets you down you do not become involved in contracts you cannot fulfil or the problems of the responses going astray in the post. You need to check out what rights customers might acquire against you under the Newspaper Publishers Association's Mail Order Protection Scheme or the Code of Practice of the Association of Mail Order Publishers. You may have to satisfy the publishers as to your suitability before being permitted to sell 'off the page'. Otherwise – and it may be the preferred style on some occasions – the advertisement could invite enquiry to which the response would be the issue of a catalogue or brochure.

When designing the advertisement or brochure it is helpful to study the good and the bad practices of those who have done it before; this is especially a good idea if you are not engaging an advertising agent. However, be careful not to breach anyone else's copyright by using their picture or quotation without their permission. Breaching someone's registered trade mark could be particularly expensive and could threaten not only your growth plans but the entire firm. In addition to awarding damages the courts are empowered to order the destruction of the goods carrying the trade mark in question. Beore going into print you should check the Trade Mark Register as not only your own errors but those of your suppliers may unwittingly lead you to a breach.

Advertisers and direct mail sellers may, through 'false' trade descriptions, attract criminal sanctions (Trade Descriptions Acts 1968/72). Competitions as a way of stimulating sales are lawful only if not contravening the Lotteries and Amusements Act 1976 and so advertisements and mail shots including competition entry forms need to be considered in the light of this Act. Finally, the Mail Order Transactions (Information) Order 1976 specifies that certain information relating to the party conducting a mail order business must be incorporated in most mail order advertisements.

## Will growth be achieved by purchasing an existing business?

In this instance it is especially important to have a good 'business' solicitor on your side. Most small business acquisitions involve a direct contract between the firm and the vendors, in the case of a limited company its shareholders. The purchase may be of the assets or the shares. The latter is appropriate if you are seeking the entire business and there is no potentially large tax liability. If the acquired company has valuable long-term contracts, these will continue and provide the basis of the planned expansion. It may also give you the size you require to assemble the right management structure and team. If instead you purchase the assets only you leave the liabilities to the vendors.

Goodwill is an important asset and you must, through the sale agreement, prevent this from being eroded by the vendors setting up in competition against you. These so-called 'contracts in restraint of trade' (or non-competition agreements) must be reasonable otherwise they become unenforceable. In a similar way you may, once again subject to legal advice, seek to prevent former employees from competing with you after leaving your service, but remember to be reasonable.

## Will your growth be based on a new product, process, material or mechanism?

### Patents

Although growth is frequently based on being 'different', or having new approaches, a small firm may be well placed to base expansion on patents or imaginative switches in convention. If the new product or process is novel, involves an inventive step and is capable of industrial application a patent could be sought. However, the Patents Act 1977 makes no provision for scientific theories, literary, dramatic and artistic works, mathematical methods or computer programs. Advice on the application can be obtained from the Patent Office, the Institute of Patentees, or a chartered patent agent.

If the application succeeds the patent continues for 20 years from the date of filing the application but it will lapse if the annual renewal fee is not paid. The 20 years allows you, as the innovator, to reap the rewards of your innovation but the extent of your 'monopoly' power will be limited if there are close substitutes. Inventions by employees during their employment may belong to you but rules exist to cover these situations and every case turns on its own facts.

Your biggest problem as a small firm will be the cost of enforcing your patent, especially when the challenge comes from a large firm. Incidentally, one way of increasing your income, especially where your resources are limited, is to sell or license your patent or manufacturing expertise to foreigners. You will, however, need a carefully worded licence agreement. Your starting point for advice, both legal and commercial, might well be the British Overseas Trade Board.

11

## Registered designs

This is a means whereby you can protect the appearance or style of your product against those seeking to imitate you. For this purpose, the method or principle of construction is irrelevant as these issues are 'judged solely by the eye'. If your production runs using any one design do not exceed 50 you can secure no protection in this way, but if on expansion your production runs exceed 50 then you may register your designs. Registration will give you exclusive use of the designs. The Register of Designs is available for public inspection.

## Trade marks

If the firm's expansion is linked to the creation of a corporate image or house style then you should register the logo, sign, mark or word that gives the product/service or firm its identity. You will be less unobtrusive as you grow, possibly into new territories, and registration is something that you may not have thought about or considered appropriate at the start-up stage. Large concerns have been known to spend millions promoting five letter words (e.g. Gleem).

The growing firm should inspect the register before beginning to nurture goodwill around a name or a logo which has to be abandoned when the registered holder learns of the situation. Apart from the wasted effort damages and costs may have to be paid.

The early registration of your trade mark is advised if you plan growth. Not only will you get the commercial value resulting from selling your product or service, but once you own a trade mark you can sell it. The goodwill value of your business may be increased greatly as a result.

## Copyright

Authors of original published material and artists rely upon copyright laws for protection. Major new legislation, the Copyright, Designs and Patents Act, comes into force later this year.

## Useful addresses

Patents, The British Library, Science Reference & Information Section, 25 Southampton Buildings, London WC2 1AY.
The Patent Office – Trade Marks – Registered Designs, State House, 66–71 High Holborn, London WC1R 4TP.

# 12   Insurance and growth

Can you identify any new risks? □ The value of insurance to the growing firm □ How much insurance should you buy? □ How should you buy insurance? □ How can David match Goliath? □ Pensions □ Life assurance □ Checklists

## How 'pure' are your 'growth' risks?

All businesses face speculative risks where the outcome ranges from loss to gain. Businesses should respond to these risks (e.g. overstocking, being eased out by competitors) by adopting appropriate business practices. Many of these practices, e.g. stock control, market research, etc., have been described in this book. One response *not* available in connection with such risks is insurance. Instead business owners must rely on sound management. Otherwise insurance against business failure would be just a method whereby well-managed efficient firms would subsidize the poorly managed. In any event efficient firms would not be drawn into such a scheme.

However, there are other risks known as pure risks where there is no prospect of gain and the position is either status quo or loss. These risks, (e.g. fire) strike at random and are as likely to hit the well-managed developing firm as any other.

## Can you identify any 'new' risks?

Insurance is a common response to such risks. It should be seen by you as a part of your risk and financial management to be reviewed in the light of your growth plans. The nature of your proposed expansion will affect the ways in which the insurace programme needs to be updated. Increased activities will increase your risk exposure. The following examples are intended to help focus your attention on some matters of importance.

## Expansion may necessitate increased investment in fixed and current assets

Sums insured on property will have to represent the full values at risk if the penalties for underinsurance are to be avoided. New forms of property and property at new locations should be brought within the policy description.

## Increase in the number of staff

The size of the payroll is particularly important to your liability insurers and increases (or decreases) are generally communicated by means of annual declarations at the end of each period of insurance. 'New' categories of employee should be notified immediately to liability insurers. Also, if not previously introduced, consideration should be given to setting up a pension scheme.

## New activities

If these affect the business description, as currently shown by the insurers, then updating is necessary. If these activities introduce higher risk exposures it may be necessary to seek the removal or modification of restrictive conditions or endorsements. These may arise under a variety of policies. In employers' liability insurance, for example, you might find, if you are in the construction industry, a clause excluding work above a certain height, e.g. 25 feet. Your new activities may result in work now being undertaken at greater heights.

## New products

It will be particularly important to ensure that your product range, as described in your products liability policy, is suitably amended. Also such policies often require you to notify, at any time, changes in risk. Consequently, even if there is no change in the product, changes in production methods will have to be notified.

## New markets

Some policies contain geographical restrictions, e.g. products liability policies may exclude exports to the USA. Check all of your liability policies carefully and compare the cover given with your exposure to overseas risks. It will be important not only to have cover on products going abroad, but account should be taken of business trips and employment of personnel, temporary or otherwise, in foreign locations.

## New contracts

These should be vetted to see how, if at all, responsibility for certain kinds of losses and liabilities is shifted. Look also to see if any obligation to insure arises. Such matters will be important not only in trading contracts but also hire purchase and leasing agreements.

## The value of insurance to the growing small firm

Whatever the nature of your expansion give your broker full details and keep a record of the information supplied. It is unlikely that you could embark on growth without insurance which enables you to convert losses (potentially large ones) unknown in amount and timing into the certainty of smaller but fixed annual costs incurred at a known time. This risk transfer facility gives you the advantages in the following areas:

(a) *Cash flow forecasting*. Premiums can be built into cash flow forecasts whereas losses uncertain in amount and timing cannot.

(b) *Pricing and costing*. The known cost of insurance can be taken into account. Without insurance, potential losses from pure risk may be ignored or become the subject of a crude estimate. If the latter is excessive, your competitive position could suffer.

The value of insurance lies in the fact that it often minimizes the cost of reaction to the risks associated with growth. After all, the alternative to the stream of revenues that may arise from new premises, new products or new markets might be to avoid the opportunities. For example, the expansion might be based on exports to the USA where the liability for injury caused by defective products is of enormous potential. The insurance premium, if at an acceptable level, opens the door to a profitable market. In all cases you have to weigh the cost of extra insurance against the extra benefits. Unfortunately many small firms evaluate their insurance only by comparing premiums with claims.

## How much insurance should you buy?

Like all costs, the cost of insurance needs to be controlled. Large concerns are able to carry some risks themselves. Fewer such opportunities arise for small firms, especially as insurance, a system of risk transfer, is unique and not easily substituted. However, a small firm should consider its potential losses, identifying those where there is a spread of risk and where the maximum loss is small. These are capable of being carried by the small firm provided that such losses can be met out of working capital without impairing the efficiency of the firm.

It is difficult to achieve the necessary spread of risk, but suppose growth means increasing the vehicle fleet from five to ten. In such circumstances special fleet rating might be available from a motor insurer and some small firms have been known to reduce cover on goods vehicles from comprehensive to third party fire and theft on such occasions. In any event you may decide under a comprehensive policy to carry the first £100 of accidental damage to your vehicle in return for a premium saving.

A managing director with a permanent health insurance policy may feel that the saving achieved by a policy providing no benefit for the first thirteen weeks of disablement from working but insuring all subsequent disablement up to a predetermined age (e.g. 65) is worthwhile. The premium saving is significant and the director has to accept 'small' losses but the really damaging 'losses' are covered.

Risk prevention and improvement can be independent of, or combined with, insurance. Despite the sophistication of modern banking methods there are still employers who pay in cash. The risk of theft in transit is removed by changing the method of payment and, if growth means a bigger payroll, the change assumes greater importance. Insurers can often give credit for good risk prevention.

## How should you buy insurance?

Business owners do not benefit from the 'consumer' protection measures of the Insurance Ombudsman Bureau, the Personal Insurance Arbitration Service and the Association of British Insurers Statements of Practice. The small business owner is treated, in this respect, as being as capable in insurance matters as ICI. Consequently your insurance needs to be purchased with some care. The insurance industry in this country has a good track record but how much better to be able to claim your protection as a matter of right rather than calling upon goodwill or generosity of insurers. You are advised to:

(a)  Purchase insurance through an insurance broker. Brokers have to be registered, follow a code of conduct and carry professional indemnity insurance. No other intermediaries are controlled in this way.

(b)  Choose the right broker, one who values your custom and understands your business. Your trade association's broker may have negotiated favourable terms.

(c)  Check the accuracy of any proposal form that you sign as you 'warrant' the accuracy of your statements.

(d)  Keep copies of all proposal forms that you sign and all other means whereby you communicate information to your insurer or broker. Review the proposals each time you renew the policies and advise the insurers of changes that have occurred.

(e)  Ensure that sums insured and limits of indemnity are adequate.

(f)  If expansion means acquiring another firm keep details of their insurance records, especially liability policies, as 'late claims' (e.g. asbestosis and other latent diseases) sometimes occur. If records are incomplete ask your broker to arrange retrospective cover.

(g)  Remember that certain insurances are compulsory by statute (third party injury/damage caused by motor vehicles and employers' liability). Others may be imposed by contract or leases but prudence usually calls for much more. Work through a comprehensive checklist with your broker.

(h)  Establish a good internal information system to ensure that you can comply with the notification and disclosure requirements of the insurer.

## How can David match Goliath?

As the business expands it may become more complex and increase your exposure to risk in the contentious areas of industrial relations, health and safety, VAT, contract disputes, etc. In effect the risk of incurring legal expenses increases while it does not become any easier to keep abreast of the law. As a result legal expenses insurances are becoming more popular.

Such policies cover legal defence costs and the attendance of witnesses at prosecutions, but will not, of course, cover fines. Cover is provided on a modular basis but all firms would be advised to consider the cover available for contract disputes. Legal expenses up to, say, £50,000 are available to pursue claims against others and to defend claims against you by others. A small firm in dispute with a large firm faced with uncertain outcome and costs might easily sacrifice its legal rights. The policy evens up this David and Goliath situation. You will also be disadvantaged if a similar sized firm, with whom you are in dispute, has such cover and you have not. Premiums are reasonable and some insurers also include a 24 hour legal advice service.

## Pensions

Pension schemes are complicated affairs for which specialist advice is required. Relatively few small business owners arrange pensions for themselves or their staff during the existence (or even survival) stage. The earlier that pension schemes can be set up the better but in any event, as with many other things, growth is an important time to review the situation. The growth process can be enhanced when a pension scheme is in place. Growth for many will mean retaining the existing labour force and attracting new staff. A pension scheme will contribute, especially in the matter of retaining the loyalty of older key staff who are likely to be very interested in pension rights. However, employees are now permitted to choose a personal pension rather join the company scheme.

For small companies (not partnerships), proposing a pension scheme for not more than twelve members, the choice will probably lie between an 'insured' pension scheme or 'small self-administered scheme' (SSA). The former, underwritten by an insurance company, has certain attractions, e.g. the insurer will have experience in the administration and investment aspects and be prepared to cope with unforeseen strain by the longevity of those receiving pensions. However, the SSA version can be established by controlling directors for their own benefit as well as that of their families and staff with a view to retaining control over the monies invested. There is considerable flexibility in the investment of and access to the funds of the scheme.

SSA schemes are becoming of increasing importance in small company growth. The particular advantages of SSA schemes compared with other schemes for the growing company are as follows:

(a) *Greater control over investment of the fund.* For example:
   (i) the fund can acquire shares in the company;
   (ii) loans as much as 50% of the fund's assets can be made to the company on a commercial basis;
   (iii) the fund can purchase commercial property including that occupied by the company.

(b) *Flexibility.* In addition to the trustees appointed by the company, there must be a pensions professional (e.g. an actuary) whose appointment is also controlled by the company. Not being tied to an insurance company the contributions can be related to cash flow considerations.

(c) *Cost.* Usually the cost will be less than that of an insured scheme but SSA works best when £10,000 or more is the annual contribution to the fund. However, if the growth prospects are such that this level of contribution can be anticipated in the future, a 'deferred' SSA can be arranged as a result of ingenious schemes offered by a limited number of large insurers.

All approved pension schemes attract excellent tax advantages. However, SSA gives benefits in the matter of inheritance tax that no insured scheme can match as benefits payable on death in service can escape the tax when written under trust. As indicated specialist advice should be sought and the adviser will need to have a clear picture of the growth plans in order that the importance of the fund as a source of finance may be properly considered.

## Life assurance

Small business owners can secure life assurance benefits for their dependants in the event of death in service by taking options available under insured pension schemes. In effect group life assurance benefits can be grafted on to pension schemes for staff, subject to Inland Revenue rules. Group life assurance is not generally expensive and will help the employer to fulfil any moral obligations to the families of staff dying in service. The small business owner will undoubtedly be key to the growth plans, and his or her premature death will put the growth and the business at risk. In the early days of growth the life assurance emphasis is more likely to be on protection than investment.

If expansion takes place by taking on new partners then you will need advice on partnership assurance. If a partner dies money will be withdrawn from the business and this may mean having to sell off assets of the business or rushing to find a new partner. The only certain way of getting money into the right hands at the right time is partnership assurance, a matter upon which, as with other life assurance aspects, your insurance broker should be consulted.

## Checklists

## Insurance and risk management

1. Identify risks by reviewing your business assets, activities and personnel and the effects of proposed expansion.
2. Check your financial statements to identify sources of loss.
3. Prepare a flow chart of all operations and activities in the larger business to identify loss possibility situations.
4. Evaluate and analyse the risks by considering the likely impact of potential losses on the business.
5. Decide how to handle or control these risks whether by avoidance, prevention, assumption or insurance. Discuss your findings with your insurance broker. Consider the advice given and work out an insurance programme that includes:

(a) all compulsory insurances (whether by statute or contract);
(b) all essential insurances (those necessary to ensure the firm's survival);
(c) all desirable insurances (losses that would disrupt the business but not necessarily destroy it).

Other available insurances may be included, even if the losses are less severe and do not pose serious threats, if you wish to have the advantage of paying a fixed sum at a stated time. Also you may value the ancillary services (e.g. advice and claims handling) of the insurer.

6. Administer risk prevention measures and keep good insurance/ accident records.

## Pensions

1. Do you already have a pension scheme for staff and/or directors?
2. How do your 'fringe' benefits (or those you propose) compare with those offered by similar firms who recruit the same type of labour?
3. What action, if any, do you consider is necessary to ensure that your growth plans are not hindered due to loss of staff or inability to recruit?
4. Have you taken specialist advice?
5. How much can you afford by way of contributions?
6. When does your first member retire?
7. Do you wish to have a directors scheme with not more than twelve members?
8. Do you understand the differences in flexibility, control and inheritance tax between a small self-administered scheme and an insured scheme?
9. Has your adviser taken steps to ensure that your scheme for directors and/or staff has been 'approved' in order to attract the tax advantages?
10. Have you taken advice on 'contracting out' of SERPS (state earnings related pension scheme)?

# Life assurance

---

1. How would your growth plans be affected by your premature death?
2. Have you tried to evaluate your needs for protection and investment and their relative importance at this stage?
3. Have you taken into account the life assurance available under any pension schemes that have been arranged or planned?
4. Besides yourself, are there any other 'key' persons whose death would seriously affect the company's future or put at risk projects in which heavy investment has been made and would need to be repeated with new personnel?
5. Have you got existing endowment policies which could provide security for loans to assist the financing of growth?
6. If you have partners or are taking on new partners have you taken advice on partnership assurance?
7. Have you consulted your insurance broker and other professional advisers?

---

12

# 13 Managing the organization

Choosing the right person □ The team □ Leadership □ Training □ Employing people □ Wages, tax and National Insurance □ Summary

It has been stated throughout this book that growth is about increasing profits and that this can be achieved by making the best possible use of all the company's resources. The most important resource of your organization is its people, therefore if any expansion plan is to succeed it is important to create the right management structure and to design and implement a general manpower plan.

A common problem in small businesses is that the owner/manager gets too closely involved in jobs which are not appropriate, for instance spending a great deal of time supervising production. Much relates to the early days of the business when he or she had to do most of the work. Even when specialist managers have been recruited it is difficult to pass over the responsibility and authority. There is often concern that employees will not show the same degree of commitment.

Owner/managers need time to think and plan, therefore you must eventually recruit a manager or managers with specialist skills such as marketing, production or accountancy, so that responsibility for some of these areas can be delegated. The introduction of new blood will bring with it a degree of dynamism which should accelerate growth.

## Choosing the right person

However, the cost of recruiting a new manager is an important consideration, not only in terms of salary but also the facilities required such as accommodation and administration. The cost of one new member of staff involves quite a high percentage increase in fixed costs, therefore the staffing plan must be an important consideration within the general financial plan, since it can affect costing, cash flow, and sources of funds.

Recruitment of specialist or managerial staff is difficult and time consuming for the small company, and more so when there is a general shortage of skills in the market-place. A small business requires managers with a more practical approach, i.e. people who are clear-headed thinkers, and who can maintain enthusiasm and driving pace. A new layer of management in a small firm brings about a ripple throughout the organization, therefore it is crucial to get the recruitment right. Since one extra person can represent a large percentage of your company, that person's abilities, behaviour and attitudes will have a greater impact on the rest of the staff than it would in a big company.

John Holt, managing director of Global Castors, feels strongly that small firms are good at employing staff. 'I believe we get it right because we can't afford not to.' He recently took the risk of employing a young graduate straight from university to take on a senior marketing post. The move involved taking a calculated risk in delegating a large proportion of the marketing exercise to someone with little experience, but who appeared to 'fit' the organization in terms of personality and ability. It worked.

The first step is to define the job, its scope, the talents and skills needed, and the reward offered. It is not easy to define a management post in a growing organization since the nature of the job is bound to change. The following list should help in designing a job description.

- Decide on the job title and state the place of work.
- List the overall objectives and purpose of the job, e.g. to ensure the profitable development of marketing operations.
- List the resources employed in the business – premises, plant, staff. State the assets he or she will control.
- Outline which of the personnel the new manager will be responsible for and to.
- List the limits of authority and key result areas.
- Describe the qualities required, e.g. technical expertise, handling people, ability to communicate, etc.

13

In view of the time needed and the importance of getting it right, the most effective approach to the recruitment of managers is to use a specialist firm of consultants to sift and reduce the list of applicants to the final few. These should then be interviewed by you and other staff on a whole day basis, rather than just by a single interview.

Recruitment of managerial staff may come from internal promotion. A member of staff who has shown leadership qualities and has the knowledge and expertise required, or who is highly motivated and keen to be trained, may prove the most suitable candidate. However, it would be unwise to consider awarding a management position to someone simply on the basis of long loyal service. It would be more sensible to reward that person with a pay rise or some other form of recognition.

## The team

For a manager there is a great deal of job satisfaction in working in a small company. Because there is closer involvement in all areas, managers tend to get a better feel for staff relationships and therefore are better able to respond to problems more effectively. There is usually a greater degree of freedom and more involvement in policy decisions than in a big company, but often the lack of real promotional prospects can become a main drawback.

Your job as leader of the organization must be to see that management operates as a team, and that the rest of the company feels part of that team. In this way you will create a culture and atmosphere within the business which is geared towards high levels of staff motivation and commitment. Each member has a range of skills and specialist knowledge which together can develop the company. Secondly, there must be real delegation of authority and responsibility; this means resisting the desire to 'help' or interfere every time there is a problem. Thirdly, when a manager is successful this should be clearly appreciated and communicated.

The team must be directed towards the company objectives. This can be brought about by providing a sense of involvement and ownership. Hold team meetings and encourage members of the organization to attend and contribute to critical decisions. Then they will all be interested in putting the decisions into action.

## Leadership

Chapter 1 talked about 'vision'. As the leader of an organization you must have vision of where you plan to take the company. Now you must convey this idea by simple and direct communication to everyone in the company, again and again. Your aim is to get every person working towards the same objective. Ray Kroc of McDonalds summed up this passion towards his company objectives: 'You've gotta see the beauty in a hamburger bun.'

'Our organization is about people – we are people oriented, without them we're sunk.' These are the words of Ken Allen, managing director of Jardinerie, a highly successful garden centre, whose total philosophy is that if people work in an atmosphere of trust, where mutual objectives are understood, they will be self-motivated to achieve. 'We have no secrets in our company, everyone knows what we are seeking to achieve, everyone expects to contribute – we operate as a team.'

Small businesses produce a higher quality, more personalized service than large entities, an aspect sorely envied by large organizations, and one you will seek to retain as your business grows. By splitting the workforce into small groups and giving each group exceptional autonomy you will retain the team approach which is so successful in the small firm. People need to work in an environment which is challenging and fun, and where they will be properly rewarded for their performance. When a small group is given a task and trusted to solve it, they will listen better and move faster. Output per employee increases and you will find that the team develops a sense of ownership. This ownership is a vital part of the equation. All the staff should be encouraged to contribute ideas on product improvement, production, work conditions, etc.

## Are you a leader?

A leader is responsible for making things happen. He or she must be dynamic, capable of creating a climate where change is acceptable and expected, and where individuals have a sense of worth. The owner/manager is the leader of the whole organization and may have a different leadership role from the managers of each section or from the leaders within small groups.

Research has shown that the qualities of leadership do not belong to a particular type of personality, i.e. leaders are not necessarily extrovert or introvert, or of a particular brand of public school. A leader is someone who knows what he or she wishes the company to achieve, and is prepared to give attention to all the details of execution. Every aspect of the business is important and interesting, and the leader is equally comfortable in executing the day-to-day tasks as in planning long-term activities. The owner/manager has outside responsibilities too, since much of the business involves customers, suppliers, authorities, shareholders and professional advisers.

13

As a manager you need to give attention to the surroundings of your staff. Pay attention to detail – see that chairs are comfortable, that colours are pleasant and cheerful, that people are not sitting in a draught. Make sure that you actually like your staff, and convey respect for them as individuals. Be reasonably firm, and take discipline seriously, but refrain from hardness or being too soft, a difficult line to find. Never discipline in front of others, and never humiliate or abuse at any time.

One of the most important qualities of a leader is the ability to listen. People who really listen convey a sense of caring. Talking to staff at all levels and allowing them to tell you about work (and personal) problems is very constructive. Firstly, you will understand changes in performance and secondly, staff relationships will be strengthened.

Do you and your management team have leadership qualities? Test yourselves against the following list (which, it must be added, is not exhaustive):

| Leader | Non-leader |
|---|---|
| • You know the names of all the people in the organization. | • You can't remember their names. |
| • You can make a decision quickly. | • You call committees. You can't decide without long debate. |
| • You delegate important work. | • You interfere, or you can't trust a whole job to anyone. |
| • You give praise. | • You never praise but are quick to take credit. |
| • You keep paperwork to a minimum. | • Every decision involves volumes of paperwork. You are 'report' oriented. |
| • You are available, and you are a good listener. | • You are never around, or when you are, you are a good talker. |
| • You will join in any aspect of work when necessary. | • You won't get your hands soiled. |
| • You admit your own mistakes, use them as a vehicle for learning. | • You never make mistakes. |
| • You keep controls to a minimum. | • The word 'control' features high in your vocabulary. |

Remember, too, that employees are good 'boss watchers'. If you wish to convey that an objective is important you must believe in it thoroughly. Your actions and body language will be closely observed, and any lack of consistency on your part will affect their performance.

There are numerous books written on the subject of leadership; many are theoretical and directed at students of behavioural science. However, one book, *In Search of Excellence* by Tom Peters and Robert Waterman, is thoroughly recommended reading for any owner/manager or aspiring leader.

## Training

Business expansion usually brings with it a need to introduce new skills to the business. Some of these skills can be acquired by training existing staff, others by recruiting specialist staff, and in some cases by recruiting and training new staff. In a small company the owner-manager is likely to be aware of skills shortages, nevertheless, a systematic approach to assessing training needs will reveal the true skills of existing staff, their aspirations for the future, and the real needs of the company. It will also help in planning staff levels and costs, and the cost of training.

Start by calling a meeting of key people, managers of sections and leaders of small groups. Ask for their contributions on the skills available within their sections and what new skills are required for the future. Which people will be affected by the changes, who should be trained, and how should the training be undertaken? If new employees are recruited can they be trained 'on the job', and if so who will undertake this? Do you have the skills to do it?

Delegation should also be a subject for discussion. Is there sufficient delegation which leaves senior managers time to think and plan? Who would be affected by greater delegation, and would further training help the process?

On-the-job training for new and existing staff undertaken by group leaders is very effective. The trainees are in a situation where they can receive constructive advice and feedback, while actually doing the job 'for real'. The leaders are in a position to communicate the organization's values, and patiently develop the skills needed. Other training may be undertaken by 'buying in' specialist training, e.g. in sales or computer skills. Perhaps some staff might need or ask to attend courses for professional qualifications.

There are a number of bodies who will give help and advice on training for your staff. Your firm may be within the scope of an Industrial Training Board who will give you information of their grant schemes for training. Alternatively, training arrangements and grants are often organized by employers' associations. Many smaller firms join a Group Training Association so that they can share the cost and administration of training with other employers. The Training Agency (formerly the Manpower Services Commission) also runs Employment Training (ET) schemes.

The Training Agency's latest contribution is one that should be of interest to most growth-minded companies. A package of services launched on 1 April 1989 called Business Growth Training is intended to help employers improve the training and development of their employees. The package seeks to meet the needs of smaller and medium-sized firms at each stage of their development. The principal aspects of the scheme are that:

- It helps fund training consultancy for firms with fewer than 500 employees. Up to 50 per cent of the costs can be made available subject to a maximum of £15,000. With this assistance firms should be able to develop a training strategy, plan the training of employees and managers, and purchase open learning materials.

- It helps disseminate new training approaches which make effective contributions to business success. Up to 50 per cent of the costs (with a maximum of £60,000) will be available for demonstration projects that show how these innovative approaches to training can be applied.
- It helps groups of employers to identify and define their key skill requirements and devise a strategy to meet them. Up to 50 per cent of the cost is available (subject to a maximum of £60,000) for selected projects.
- New and other small businesses will be able to secure training for their owners and managers to assist in the development of the skills needed to enable them develop and run their companies.

You would be well-advised to secure the government's free guide on the scheme, *People, Performance and Profit*, which includes a checklist to assist you to review and adapt your current investment in people in the light of your future business objectives.

## Employing people

This section sums up the minimum legal requirements for employment while *Hiring and Firing* by Karen Lanz, published in this series, deals with the subject in detail.

A small expanding business may take on enough extra staff, or fully-employed staff for the first time, and now needs to develop good personnel practices. A number of personnel issues and problems are likely to occur, and it is increasingly important to gain information in these matters.

### Finding suitable employees

When advertising vacancies and interviewing for staff you must keep in mind that the job must be open to both sexes and all races. You may be exempt from the sex discrimination law if you employ less than 6 people, but not from that on race. When you employ more than 20 people, at least 3 per cent of your workforce must be registered disabled unless you are unable to fulfil your quota, in which case the local job centre will advise you further.

### Contracts of employment

A person starting work with your firm enters into a legal contract with you straight away. However, a written statement of the main terms and conditions of their employment must be provided by you for employees who work more than 16 hours a week, within 13 weeks. This will include your name, the exact date on which employment began, the job title, rate of pay, hours of work, holiday provision, pensions, sick pay, length of notice, disciplinary rules, and grievance procedures. Should any of these terms and conditions change you must tell the employee in writing within a month of the change. A contract of employment must be drawn up for an employee who has worked for you for more than 8 hours a week for over 5 years.

The contract of employment lets everyone know where they stand. You may include more than the statutory requirements in the written statement if you wish.

## Wages, tax and National Insurance

You must give your employees statements of gross pay, itemized deductions and take home pay. If employing people for the first time you must tell the local tax office who will furnish you with all the required stationery and information for the deduction of PAYE. You are also responsible for deducting Class 1 National Insurance from the employee, and for making employer's contributions to National Insurance. The local Department of Social Security will give you advice on state pension schemes and an insurance broker can advise on private pension schemes.

In deciding on the rate of pay, you should take into account any national and local union agreements, statutory minimum rates laid down by Wages Councils if these apply, and the 'going rate' for the job. Men and women who are employed on 'like work', or work rated as equivalent, must be afforded equal treatment in terms and conditions.

13

### Hours of work and leave of absence

There are limits on the hours which can be worked within a certain period for some occupations, e.g. driving. Shop assistants and women and young people under 18 employed in industry are also subject to certain restrictions in hours.

Employees have a right to time off for attending ante-natal clinics, trade union activities, or public duties. There are also certain rights afforded to pregnant women with reference to time off and returning to work within a stated time scale.

## Health and safety

If you employ five or more people you must prepare a written statement on your policy regarding the health and safety of your employees and of the organization, and arrangements for carrying it out.

You may be required to insure against liability for bodily injury or disease sustained by employees and arising out of or in the course of their employment.

## Short-time working and guarantee payments

Your expansion plans may not materialize in quite the way you expected. There may be a situation where a fall in orders means there is not enough work, and you will need to lay off workers on a temporary basis in order to ease cash flow. The law has made some basic provisions to protect your employees. You must pay them a 'guarantee payment' of a fixed minimum daily amount, and this is limited to five days in any three month period.

## Discipline and dismissals

When a disciplinary problem arises, the written rules and procedures, previously agreed with employees (and unions, if involved) should be followed. You should make it clear who has authority to deal with the problem, and what course of action will be taken. Anyone with a complaint should have a chance to be, and can be accompanied by a fellow employee or union representative at disciplinary hearings. There should also be rights of appeal.

Oral and written warnings should be given before a dismissal, and careful records should be kept. Anyone who has worked for you for more than 6 months can ask for a written statement of the reasons for dismissal within 14 days. Most employees can make a complaint of unfair dismissal to an industrial tribunal within 3 months of leaving work if they have had one year of continuous service.

## Summary

People are the most important resource in your organization. Owner/managers will need to design a proper manpower plan for the next phase of growth. All too often the owner/manager is too busy running the business to find time for planning the future, and therefore may need to recruit further management help.

Extra management staff will cause changes throughout the business. The cost of a new member of staff is a high proportion of all the costs, and therefore must feature in the financial plan. Define the job and its objectives, then decide on the qualities required. Recruitment may be internal or external; the most important aspect is that the candidate 'fits' the organization.

The owner/manager must see that management operates as a team, whose objective is to develop the company. He or she has special leadership responsibilities within the company, and also outside with shareholders, customers, professional bodies, etc. Leadership is based on having a vision of where you plan to take the company, and having the dedication to motivate others to this end. Leaders have no specific type of personality. A leader has the ability to listen to people and to care about them. Small businesses produce a higher quality, more personalized service than large entities, an aspect they will seek to retain as the business grows.

People need to work in an environment which is challenging and fun, and where they will be properly rewarded for their performance. Most growing businesses need to introduce new skills; some of these can be gained by training. You will need to assess training needs for your company. On the job training means that the trainee can do the job 'for real', and receive constructive advice and feedback. There are a number of bodies who will give help and advice on training for your staff.

A growing business taking on extra staff will need to develop good personnel practices.

1

# Index